Dark Way to Paradise

Dark Way
To Paradise

Dante's Inferno *in*
Light of the Spiritual Path

by
Jennifer Doane Upton

edited by
Charles S. Upton

SOPHIA PERENNIS

HILLSDALE NY

First published in the USA
By Sophia Perennis
Series editor: James R. Wetmore
© Jennifer Doane Upton 2004

Series editor: James R. Wetmore

For information, address:
Sophia Perennis, P.O. Box 611
Hillsdale NY 12529
sophiaperennis.com

Printed in the United States of America

Library of Congress Cataloging-in-Publication Data

Upton, Jennifer D.
Dark way to paradise: Dante's Inferno in light
of the spiritual path / Jennifer D. Upton.

p. cm.

Includes bibliographical references and index.
ISBN 1-59731-001-8 (pbk: alk. paper)
ISBN 1-59731-009-3 (cloth: alk. paper)
1. Hell. 2. Conversion. 3. Spiritual Life.
4. Dante Alighieri, 1265–1321. Inferno.
I. Title.
BT 836.3. U68 2004
851'.1—dc22   2004021366

I dedicate this book to Alvin Moore, Jnr.
whose own reading of Dante has been a
constant inspiration

We could not live in Paradise
Looking on those in Hell
Without remaking them in our own world;
For what we would see would not be Hell,
But the Paradise of another god.

—J. D. U

Acknowledgements

MANY PEOPLE HAVE HELPED me in the writing of this book. In particular I would like to thank Darryl Jones, for showing me that it is possible to read Dante in light of the Church Fathers; Lawrence Meehan, for his personal support and willingness to post some of the material that went into this book on his website; Alvin Moore, for his substantive and ongoing encouragement; my husband Charles, for helping me organize the material, for his many ideas, his editing of the final manuscript, and for the majority of the footnotes; and Dr. Rama Coomaraswamy, for his sincere support during those times when I feared I might not have the spirit to complete this project.

While working on my exegesis of Dante's *Inferno*, I relied on the verse translation of Allen Mandelbaum, from his *The Divine Comedy of Dante Aligheri* (NY: Bantam Books, 1982), which I admire for its clarity. However, copyright considerations made it necessary to insert a copyright-free translation prior to publication. For this I turned to Longfellow's translation. But since Longfellow's language is stilted and archaic in places, and sometimes nearly impossible to understand, my husband took it upon himself to re-write nearly half of the quoted text, relying largely on the literal meaning of Mandelbaum's translation, while also consulting the translations of Laurence Binyon and Lawrence Grant White. This explains the rather hybrid nature of the verse, where sometimes 'thou' and 'dost' are used, sometimes 'you' and 'do'. We can only hope that the present version makes up, by its clarity, for whatever it may lack in terms of unity of style.

In the Introduction and once in Canto III I have included text from Laurence Binyon's translation in *The Portable Dante* (NY: The Viking Press, 1947).

CONTENTS

Foreword

JENNIFER DOANE UPTON has provided us with a remarkable study of Dante's *Inferno* that brings the often obscure text down the level of the individual soul—hers, mine, and the reader's—and this in a manner no other contemporary commentary does. I was greatly pleased to be asked to contribute a Foreword, especially as it led me to once again read the book. A practicing Orthodox Christian with a long-standing interest in psychology, and familiar with the mystical writings of other religious traditions, Mrs. Upton brings us many new insights (or perhaps reminds us of many old ones) into the *Inferno*. But make no mistake. While scholarly, this is not a scholar's text, but rather a spiritual guide to the path that each and every one of us must travel. You might say that she shares with us her own travail, and invites us to join her.

The author explains that Dante had to go through Hell in order to be convicted of his sin, to witness the darkness in his own soul. And for this, as we all do, he needed a guide, namely Virgil, whom Augustine loved to the point that he feared it might be sinful. More than a guide is required, however; we also need the virtue of hope which enables us to witness and deal with the reality of sin—our sin. Furthermore, Dante makes it clear that he could live in this hope only because of the mercy of the Blessed Virgin, who among other things symbolizes the soul—his soul and ours—in a state of grace.

I invite the reader to share the pleasures and insights of this wonderful text.

DR. RAMA P. COOMARASWAMY, MD

Preface

THE TITLE OF THIS BOOK is *Dark Way to Paradise*. But how can such a thing be? How can Hell be a road to Heaven? The souls of the blessed dead either pass through purgation or fly directly to Paradise; any departed soul which enters Hell will encounter only eternal damnation. To ask the question another way: Why must Dante go through Hell? Maximos the Confessor replies:

> [God] wishes to make the devil's power of chastisement and hatred of men the contingent cause of the return to virtue of those who by their own free choice have lapsed from it. ... The contemplative and gnostic intellect is often committed for punishment to the devil, deservedly suffering hardship and affliction at his hands. This is so that by suffering it may learn patiently to endure affliction rather than to trifle arrogantly to no purpose with things that do not exist.[1]

And Martin Lings:

> [The] descent into hell for the discovery of the soul's worst possibilities is only necessary because these possibilities are an integral part of the psychic substance and need to be recovered, purified and reintegrated, for in order to be perfect the soul must be complete.[2]

Dante must go through Hell because he is alive, which means that he is conscious on the plane of choice; he has to travel through the

---

1. 'First Century of Various Texts', paragraphs 86 and 88, from *The Philokalia, the Complete Text*, compiled by St. Nikodimos of the Holy Mountain and St. John of Corinth (London: Faber and Faber, 1990), p184.
2. *The Secret of Shakespeare* (Cambridge: Quinta Essentia, 1996), p63.

Inferno consciously. The damned, on the other hand, are those who would rather die than face their own evil. Dante, in his dark journey, does not suffer this evil more intensely than the damned do, but he does suffer the *import* of it, which is the very thing the damned are desperately trying to deny. Mercy must keep Dante at a distance from Hell even as he passes through it. This distance, however—which is in itself an existential alienation—cannot help but tempt him to identify with the more profound alienation he sees in the souls of the damned. As he descends through the circles, he and his guide Virgil nearly come into conflict over the fact that Dante tends to identify with the damned souls around him; he draws dangerously close to seeing himself as damned like they are, and so sinking into despair. Thus to find the opening to Purgatory at the bottom of Hell is a pure mercy; had Dante tried to leave Hell by the path on which he entered it, he would certainly have been lost.

Dante had to witness the damned in order to illumine the evil in his own soul—yet if he had identified with that evil, he too would have been damned. The harrowing of Hell requires spiritual hope; it takes hope to witness sin as it really is. If it were not for the mercy of the Holy Virgin, he would never have been capable of having this vision and not being destroyed by it. The vision of Hell reveals what one has to be purified of—not after death, when it is too late, but in this very life.

In traveling through the *Inferno*, Dante moves past circles of lost souls who cannot travel themselves; they are mired eternally in the form of their ruling sin. In his ascent of the Mount of Purgatory, on the other hand, he and his guide travel past toiling souls who are ascending like they are. Yet in Paradise, the souls of the blessed are once again fixed in their stations, as Dante moves past them in his ascent. What does all this mean? What is the import of it?

In Hell, the fact that the damned are incapable of movement shows that they are chained to all the sins, the fears and the angers they simply could not face in life. They weren't always directly confronted with their own evil in this life, but in Hell they are faced with it constantly, even though they themselves still cannot face it. Hell, then, is the form of willful ignorance.

The fact that the souls in Purgatory are capable of motion proves that one can indeed move away from one's own evil. A soul in purgation suffers the hardships of that evil, but without despair. The souls in the *Purgatorio* already see salvation in potential—at least through the image of the Earthly Paradise—but they must still travel toward it. Thus Purgatory is the archetype of the spiritual Path. Those in Purgatory feel a spiritual potential awakening in their souls, which moves progressively toward actualization and fulfillment. Only gradually, however, does the joy of spiritual fulfillment outweigh the tremendous suffering of purgation. When this awakening potential finally penetrates every aspect of these souls, they find themselves in the Earthly Paradise. And it is there where their real intuitions of Paradise as such begin.

Hell is the realm of privation, of relative non-existence where being itself is a burden; in the *Inferno*, materiality dominates the psyche and blots out the Spirit. Purgatory is the intermediate or *imaginal* realm, which is why Dante can dream there. And Paradise is the *intelligible* realm.

That Dante moves in the same direction as the souls in Purgatory demonstrates how after-death purgation and the struggles of a soul going through purgation in this life have a mysterious affinity. This is why it is possible for an incarnate soul to 'offer up' its sufferings in order to aid those departed souls in their posthumous ascent.

When Dante finally enters Paradise, he finds that the souls of the blessed are also fixed in their stations, like those in Hell. This fixity does not mean, however, that they do not participate in motion, only that their motion is not a reaching for some goal that is beyond them so much as a participation in the motion of Infinity, which penetrates every existence. In Hell, this inescapable motion creates oppression and restlessness; in Paradise, pure song. The fixity of the souls of the blessed—which, mysteriously, is not other than their motion—denotes not oppression but crystallization. Every soul in the *Paradiso*, from the lowest to the highest circles, participates in total perfection, and is therefore at rest.

When Dante is traveling through the *Inferno*, his ability to move demonstrates how his capacities and outlook are broader and fuller than those of the damned, who are paralyzed. But in Paradise his motion shows his state to be more limited than that of the blessed souls. Because he is still outside of Paradise in essence, though traveling through it in vision, he is close to the mystery of how the motionlessness of those souls is not paralysis, as motionlessness must often seem to us in this world, but rather contentment and peace. This paradisiacal peace is based on the fact every soul in Paradise is in intimate relation to every other; they don't have to travel to distant points to meet each other because in Paradise, where all is relation, no point is distant.

Dante, still partly bound to time, must travel, must see perfection successively because he himself is not yet perfect. This is the only way he can experience spiritual perfection before fully realizing it, and the only way he can transmit to us the intimations of it. But the souls in Paradise have no need of travel; the totality of perfection is already theirs, both now and in eternity.

Introduction

Dante's Vision of Spiritual Love

THE LOVE OF LITERATURE has been with me all my life. Coming upon Dante a few years ago, it was in the knowledge that a work like the *Divine Comedy* contains deep spiritual meaning, and was in fact written for the sake of that meaning. It ought to be unnecessary to say something so obvious, except for the fact that the way in which I read the *Divine Comedy* is exactly the opposite from the way in which a postmodern critic or 'philosopher' would read it.

Central to the way I have been reading the *Divine Comedy* is Titus Burckhardt's essay 'Because Dante is Right', from *Mirror of the Intellect, Essays on Traditional Science and Sacred Art*. Dante himself, in the *Convivio*, spoke of four levels of meaning: the literal, the allegorical, the moral, and the anagogical or mystical. Burckhardt takes a harsh view of those critics who emphasize the historical or aesthetic aspects of Dante's great poem at the expense of its spiritual meaning. He says, speaking of post-Renaissance criticism of the *Commedia*,

> excuses were made for the poet, and his artistic mastery was even credited with enabling him to bridge over poetically 'this scholastic sophistry' about multiple meanings. Thus people fundamentally misunderstood the source upon which the poet drew for his work of creation, since the multiplicity of meaning in it is not the result of a preconceived mental construction grafted onto the actual poem; it arises directly and spontaneously our of a supramental inspiration, which at one and the same time penetrates and shines through every level of the soul—the reason, as well as the imagination and the inward ear.[1]

1. Titus Burckhardt, *Mirror of the Intellect: Essays on Traditional Science and Sacred Art* (Albany: SUNY Press, 1987), pp82–83.

This means that, for Dante, the 'afterlife' portrayed in the *Comme-dia* is very real, and that most of its reality lies on levels of meaning higher than the literal.

The literal level is what is perceived through the five senses and the experiences they bring us. This is the only level that many moderns can credit with the name 'reality'. To them, stories of the state of the soul and the afterlife seem to be contained within the experience of corporeal existence, much as a dream is contained within a night's sleep. When modern critics limit their treatment of the *Commedia* to its historical, cultural and political levels of mean-ing, they confine themselves to the literal.

A materialist, in order to reinforce his argument, might say that the 'soul' along with its 'afterlife' is actually present in *this* life. After all, isn't Dante writing about people he has known and qualities he has recognized in the material world? This is true—but if the soul with its 'afterlife' is already present in terrestrial life, it is not because the level of being it represents originated in this life. Rather, the soul, through its participation in higher levels of being, includes physical existence within itself, since the greater reality necessarily encompasses the lesser. From the point of view of the soul, it is the earth that is a dream and not the other way around.

From a traditional perspective like Dante's, to ignore higher lev-els of meaning for the sake of the earthly one is to risk allowing one's soul to fall below the earthly level and into the state called 'Hell'. According to Dante, those in Hell 'have lost the good of the intellect' (*Inferno* iii:18). As Burckhardt says, 'For Dante, man's original dignity consists essentially in the gift of the 'Intellect,' by which is meant not merely the reason or the thinking faculty, but rather that ray of light that connects the reason and indeed the whole soul with the divine source of all knowledge.'[2] The damned in Hell may be 'smart' like cunning politicians and lawyers, but they have no intellectual intuition of higher realities. It is in these reali-ties, particularly the mystical one, that love and knowledge meet and are united.

2. Ibid., p87

Burckhardt sees Beatrice as a symbol of this union of love and knowledge. However, he criticizes those who would regard her merely as an allegory of wisdom. Her literal existence is also needed. He says,

> That Dante should have bestowed upon Divine Wisdom the image and name of a beautiful and noble woman is in accordance with a compelling law, not merely because Divine Wisdom, insofar as it is the object of knowledge, includes an aspect which is precisely feminine, in the highest sense, but also because the presence of the Divine *Sophia* manifests itself first and foremost to him in the appearance of the beloved woman.[3]

The beauty of Beatrice in Paradise is not like the mere physical beauty of a woman with a morally lukewarm character. Her beauty is the presence of Love itself. If, in Purgatory, Dante must go through the fire which purifies the lustful and then endure the reproaches of Beatrice, it is so that all the love within him can be tried and made strong. After all, how can he meet Love face to face if he himself is not also Love? Burckhardt says of this paradisiacal Beatrice,

> It is significant that here Dante no longer stresses the moral beauty of Beatrice—her goodness, innocence and humility—as he did in his *La Vita Nuova*, but speaks quite simply of her visible beauty; what is most outward has here become the image of what is most inward, sensory observation the expression of spiritual vision.[4]

Some may interpret this to mean, however, that Love is fully subsumed in Beauty, that aesthetic contemplation is in every case Love's highest development. But such is not necessarily the case. Beauty must serve either Truth or falsehood. Beauty that serves Truth participates in Love, which is more inclusive than beauty, whereas beauty that serves falsehood leads to the destruction of the soul. Furthermore, aesthetic appreciation and refined feeling aren't

3. Ibid., p93.
4. Ibid., p94.

always the same. There is a cold aesthetic which denies true feeling every bit as much as exterior thought does.

While Dante wrote profoundly about spiritual love, he certainly knew intimately the dangers of false love. He composed a series of poems dedicated to a woman named *Pietra*, 'stone', who totally captivates his heart even though she is cruel and in no way returns his affections. Because all the warmth in him goes out to her, but finds nothing kindred in her to respond to it, he is, through this experience, *petrified*, just as he comes close to being turned to stone by the Medusa in CANTO IX of the *Inferno*.

He is of course describing in these poems the experience of being psychologically destroyed through fascination, which is equally dangerous whether it be for a false woman or a false philosophy. What is it, then, which makes his affection for this woman so different than his love for Beatrice, who also fascinated him, and who, at least on an earthly level, did not reciprocate his feelings?

In the *Purgatorio*, Beatrice rebukes Dante for having permitted his attention to stray to other women (or false philosophies) instead of allowing it, when she died, to follow her to her grave. Superficially his attraction to the stone woman and his love for Beatrice are similar, but inwardly the difference is immense, since, through Beatrice, Dante comes face to face with Divine Mercy itself, whose archetypal symbol within the poem is the Virgin Mary. He gives his attention to that Mercy, which has given visions of the Virgin to so many — and since he has first given, he is now able to receive such grace from that Mercy, which is finally the Virgin herself, that the very darkest places in his soul are illuminated. After all, did not Beatrice, who is a substitute for the Virgin, leave her footprint in Hell? Through his vision of Beatrice, those wounds to his soul which were caused by his propensity to yield to profane fascination are healed.

At what place, and in what time, did Dante's fascination for the stone-hearted woman end, and his love for Beatrice, which is a path to Divine Love, begin? Even though Dante describes the beginning of this love in *La Vita Nuova*, the reader does not really know the true time and place of this love's awakening, because that is a secret of the soul. The true time and place of the birth of his love for Beatrice are at the point where the Divine Mercy itself came into his life and penetrated into its innermost depths. The senses do not know about this event; it is the soul alone which hears it.

There is, in contemporary society, a profound ignorance of true feeling leading to an emotional coldness which opens the soul to worldliness, even when doctrinal understanding, in its own dimension, had successfully shut that world out. This emotional coldness and ignorance are overcome through the development of true objectivity in the feeling realm.

Developed feeling is refined and subtle. Far from being merely sentimental or demonstrative, it often withholds its own demonstration when such a manifestation would destroy the context in which it appears; this explains why, while he is in the Inferno, Dante never pronounces Beatrice's name. Feeling must be cultivated, both for the sake of the fullness of human life, and because it itself, when conformed to the Intellect, can be a perfect vehicle for the union with God, not only due to the psychic energy it releases, but also because of the particular perceptions which only developed feeling can give; this is not *bhakti* as we usually think of it. There are certain avenues to the transcendent Intellect which are only open through feeling. *Paradiso* 28:1–12:

> *When she who hath imparadised my mind*
> *Hath stript the truth bare, and its contraries*
> *In the present life of wretched mortal-kind,*
> *As one who, looking in the mirror, sees*
> *A torch's flame that is behind him lit*
> *Ere in his sight, or in his thought, it is*
> *And turns to see if the glass opposite*
> *Have told him truth, and findeth it agree*
> *Therewith, as truly as note and measure fit;*
> *So is recorded in my memory*
> *That I turned, looking on those eyes of light*
> *Whence love had made the noose to capture me.*

It is habitually assumed in today's world that feeling is strictly subjective. But it is more accurate to say that some feelings are objectively true and others objectively false. If you love a demon, for example, your feelings are not *true*. The modern world revels in the passions, but in many ways it attempts to kill the 'still, small voice' of objective feeling. True feeling can often seem small and unimportant, like alpine flowers, even though these apparently in-significant plants have the power to endure great cold.

Many people today who have an interest in metaphysics tend to believe that feelings are mere 'accidents'. Yet one can lose one's soul through false feeling, while true feeling can save it, and nothing that has to do with salvation and damnation can be only accidental. In *Paradiso* 26:59–63, Dante says:

> *The Death which He, that I might live, endured*
> *And hope, whereto the faithful, as I, cling*
> *Joined with that living knowledge* [i.e., the 'bitings' of
>   Divine Love in union with human love] *have secured*
> *That from the sea of the erring love retrieved*
> *On the shore of the right love I stand assured.*

Given the belief prevailing in certain metaphysical circles that the affections are accidental, some conclude that because the feeling soul is therefore the principle of the passions and vices, including pride. But feeling is certainly no more *inherently* prideful than thought. True feeling relates to the more spiritual aspects of the soul; only false feeling is involved with the passions. And Love, which is of divine origin, pertains to more than the feeling soul. But though Love is more than feeling, it never excludes feeling; if Love is there, feeling is there. The feeling may be there obliquely; some-times one may be more objectively loving by acting against certain feelings. Nonetheless, Love is always the crown of true feeling, which means objective feeling. *Paradiso* 26:28–39:

> *. . . the good, soon as 'tis perceived as good*
> *Enkindles love and makes it more to live*
> *The more of good it can itself include.*
> *Therefore to the Essence, whose prerogative*
> *Is, that what good outside of it is known*
> *Is naught else than a light its own beams give*

More than elsewhither must in love be drawn
The mind of him whose vision can attain
The verity the proof is founded on.
This verity to my intellect is made plain
By Him who to that prime love testifies
Which all the eternal substances maintain.

Titus Burckhardt's mentor, the metaphysician Frithjof Schuon, in his book *Survey of Metaphysics and Esoterism*, presents a doctrine of the affections which throws light on that of Dante:

> Not to be 'emotional': this seems, nowadays, to be the very condition of 'objectivity', whereas in reality objectivity is independent of the presence or absence of the emotional element.... [p189] Emotivity manifests and allows one to perceive those aspects of a good or an evil which mere logical definition could not manifest directly and concretely.... In a spiritual man there is a continuity between his inward impassibility—resulting from his consciousness of the Immutable—and his emotion.... [p190] In the emotion of the spiritual man, the 'motionless mover' always remains present and accessible. As his emotion is linked to knowledge, the truth is never betrayed.... [p192] Fundamentally, we would say that where there is Truth, there is also Love. Each Deva possesses its Shakti; in the human microcosm, the feeling soul is joined to the discerning intellect, as in the Divine Order Mercy is joined to Omniscience; and as, in the final analysis, Infinitude is consubstantial with the Absolute.[5]

Go back to that old melodious phrase 'true love'. It sounds merely sentimental to us now. But 'true' equals 'objective'; true love is objective love. Many a person has reached the threshold of spiritual Truth by starting from the thinking function, only to have that Truth destroyed in his life through false feeling. True feeling, on the other hand, can be a 'homing' faculty, drawing us toward the Center almost faster than we could travel on our own initiative. In the

---

5. *Survey of Metaphysics and Esoterism* (Bloomington: World Wisdom Books, 1986), p194.

words of St. Bernard, symbol of divine contemplation, to Dante in *Paradiso* 32:149–150: 'And do thou with thy feeling [*l'affezione*] follow on/My words, that close to them thy heart [i.e., the *nous*, the spiritual Intellect] may cling.'

According to Dante, Love is the Supreme Goal of the spiritual life, not simply the energy driving it. And that supreme, objective Love is another name for the transcendent Intellect. In *Paradiso* 32:142–144, St. Bernard says:

> *And turn we to the Primal Love our eyes,*
> > *So that, still gazing toward Him, thou may'st pierce*
> > *Into His splendor, as far as in thee lies.*

And in *Paradiso* 33:85–92, Dante declares:

> *I beheld leaves within the unfathomed blaze*
> > *Into one volume bound by love, the same*
> > *That the universe holds scattered through its maze.*
> *Substance and accidents, and their modes, became*
> > *As if together fused, all in such wise*
> > *That what I speak of is one simple flame.*
> *Verily I think I saw with mine own eyes*
> > *The form that knits the whole world. . . .*

⨭

In a letter to Charles Williams, Dante scholar Dorothy Sayers complains that, although Beatrice holds a high place for Dante, he doesn't seem to occupy such an exalted place for her, at least not in terrestrial existence. Sayers feels that for the sake of justice Dante ought to have had a chance to mean for someone else what Beatrice meant for him. She sees their love as one-sided, and seems not to believe that Dante and Beatrice were ever truly united.

Perhaps, however, Sayers misses the point. At the level of Paradise, where Beatrice takes her proper place, she and Dante are so close to God that the distinction between subject and object begins to disappear. Beatrice drops out of sight in the poem not because Dante has lost touch with her, but because the burden of the subject/object distinction has been removed from them. The great Persian poet Nizami, writing of the lovers Layla and Majnun, tells of how Majnun finds a piece of paper with his name and Layla's written on it. He tears the paper in two and throws away Layla's name, but keeps his own. From that time on, no one can say Majnun's name without including Layla. Likewise, in the last part of the *Paradiso*, Dante no longer speaks of Beatrice because the very possibility of ever being apart from her has disappeared. Not talking with her and not seeing her are no longer able to bring separation.

Through virtue and beauty, Beatrice has allowed her soul to take on a substance so like that of the Virgin that there is no separation there either. When Beatrice's love and sorrow for Dante on account of his straying from the true path become so great that she goes to plead with Virgil to help him, thereby leaving her footprint in Hell, her love for Dante is not other than the love of the Virgin Mary for all mankind. Therefore, in the last part of the poem, we are shown Dante encountering, not Beatrice, but St. Bernard, who in life had simply said 'I love because I love,' and who now, in Paradise, is seen singing a hymn to the Virgin, to whom he is completely devoted. The Mother of God is she whose mercy encompasses all the heavens, until it at last becomes inseparable from 'the love that moves the sun and the other stars.'

But for Dante, the beginning of this knowledge must be his encounter, for the sake of love, with all that is against love; in order to become worthy of meeting love face-to-face, he must travel through Hell. The souls in the Inferno display the grotesqueness that comes upon them in their attempt to live against love. No matter how much they may curse and deny it, however, love impinges upon them at every moment.

Canto I

Dante finds himself in a dark wood, having lost his way. As the sun rises, he tries to climb the slope of a hill, but his way is blocked by three beasts. He turns back to the valley below, and encounters the poet Virgil, who tells him he cannot pass the She-wolf, though a savior will arise in the future, deliver Italy from her, and drive her into Hell. He tells Dante that he is to follow him through the circles of Hell and Purgatory, after which Beatrice will appear to guide him through Paradise. Dante begins his journey.

THE DIVINE COMEDY begins with the famous lines:

> *Midway upon the journey of our life*
> *I found myself within a forest dark,*
> *For the straightforward pathway had been lost.*
> *Ah me! how hard a thing it is to say*
> *What was this forest savage, rough, and stern,*
> *Which in the very thought renews the fear.*
> *So bitter is it, death is little more;*
> *But to recall the good which there I found,*
> *Speak will I of the other things I saw.* [1–9]

The following words of Maximos the Confessor perhaps describe the spiritual condition to which Dante alludes:

If he who suffers for having transgressed one of God's commandments recognizes the principle of divine providence which is healing him, he accepts the affliction with joy and gratitude, and corrects the fault for which he is being disciplined. But if he is insensitive to this treatment, he is justly deprived of the grace that was once given him and is handed over to the turbulence of the passions; he is abandoned so that he may acquire by ascetic labour those things for which he inwardly longs.[1]

Here may imagine Dante at the midpoint of his life, still successful in worldly terms, not yet in exile. The mid-point of life is the moment when, in the 'normal' course of things, the spiritual return to God should begin to predominate. Christ was crucified at the mid-point of what would have been a normal life-span in His day. This is the point where outward manifestation has reached its limit, after which a person must either ascend spiritually or be content to live within the progressive deterioration of the form of his life.

The successful part of Dante is like Dives, the name given by tradition to the rich man in Luke 16:19–31, who refused to comfort the poor man Lazarus. Lazarus dies and is carried by angels into Abraham's bosom; Dives dies as well, and finds himself in Hades. He cries out to Abraham to send Lazarus to bring him at least one drop of water, but this is impossible. He then implores Abraham to send Lazarus to warn his family to repent of their evil ways, but is told that 'If they do not hear Moses and the prophets, neither will they be convinced if some one should rise from the dead.' Dante is like a Dives who can still repent because he can see beyond time.

> *And even as he, who, with distressful breath,*
> *Forth issued from the sea upon the shore,*
> *Turns to the water perilous and gazes;*
> *So did my soul, that still was fleeing onward,*
> *Turn itself back to re-behold the pass*
> *Which never yet a living person left.*
> *After my weary body I had rested,*
> *The way resumed I on the desert slope;*
> *My firmest foot was always the one below.* [22–30]

The soul of Dante is weak; it doesn't have a firm foothold on the straight path of salvation, of return to God. His lower foot is always firmer because he is dragged down by the passions, symbolized by

---

1. *First Century of Various Texts*, from *The Philokalia*, paragraph 89, pp184–185.

the three beasts, a leopard, a lion and a wolf; he cannot ascend the Mount of Purgatory without first encountering them.

'Before mine eyes did one present himself,' says Dante, 'who seemed from long-continued silence hoarse.' [62–63]. This is Virgil, who is to be Dante's guide through Hell.

> *'Have pity on me,' unto him I cried,*
> *'Whichever thou art, shadow or real man!'*
> *'Not man,' he said, 'though human once I was,*
> *And my two parents were of Lombardy,*
> *Mantuans by country both of them.*
> Sub Julio *was I born, though it was late,*
> *And lived at Rome under the good Augustus,*
> *During the time of false and lying gods.'* [65–72]

The fact that Virgil gives Dante his history and ancestry instead of his name indicates that Dante himself will reach universality through his own particularity, including his ethnicity. (It is important to remember here that Virgil was so well loved by the Latins that St. Augustine considered his love for him to be almost sinful.) Homer may have been a greater poet than Virgil, but Virgil was *Dante's* poet: what we most truly love can most truly guide us.

Dante can see Hell only after he 'turns itself back to re-behold the pass' [22–27] after his deepest spiritual darkness is already past. How much more powerful it is to say it in this way than to glibly preach that the Path requires a spiritual death! The leopard Dante encounters is often said to symbolize lust, the lion, pride, and the she-wolf, avarice. Dante's soul is invaded by these three beasts. Because he can't yet walk the spiritual Path directly, the wolf drives him back to where 'the Sun is silent' [60]. Jesus is called the 'Sun of Righteousness'; and as Seyyed Hossein Nasr reminds us, in an interview in *Parabola* magazine [VOL. VIII, no. 4], the Sufis also call Jesus the Sun. If the Sun cannot speak, then the Word cannot fully be made flesh.

Virgil, however, provides a way around this impasse; in Hell, Dante has a guide where guidance usually cannot appear, because Hell is dispersion. When Dante says to Virgil, 'Thou art my master and my author' [85], he names him as his spiritual Guide from all eternity.

About the she-wolf, Virgil says:

'... *this beast, at which thou criest out,*
   Suffers not any one to pass her way,
   But so doth harass him, that she destroys him;
She has a nature so malign and ruthless,
   That never can she sate her greedy will,
   But after food is hungrier than before.
Many the animals with whom she mates,
   And more they shall be still, until the Greyhound
   Comes, who shall make her perish in her pain.
He shall not feed on either land or gold [literally 'pewter']
   But upon wisdom, and on love and virtue;
   Between Feltro and Feltro shall his nation be;
Of that low Italy shall he be the savior,
   On whose account the maid Camilla died,
   And Euryalus, Turnus, Nisus, of their wounds;
Through every city shall he hunt her down,
   Until he shall have driven her back to Hell,
   There from whence envy first did let her loose.' [94–110]

The Greyhound represents the Holy Roman Emperor, the secular savior Dante looks for, who will save the popes from corruption by worldly affairs and provide the nearest possible Christian equivalent to the Muslim *shari'at*. The she-wolf, destined to be overcome by the Greyhound, symbolizes not so much avarice or cupidity as *envy*—perhaps the tendency of the popes to envy the power of the secular authorities, with whom their own quasi-secular status placed them in constant rivalry, to the detriment of their purely spiritual function. According to Victor Danner,

the fact that Islam does have a sacred law covering both individual and collective life ... implies that, from the very beginning, the religion set out to distinguish itself from the Christian world around it, which had no sacred Law. ... No religion [however] can address a people without making some attempt at social legislation. [T]he Christian rejection of Jewish Law, done in the name of the mystical Way of the Christ, therefore had to become the Christian acceptance of Roman Law. The result was that the [western] Church assumed an almost anti-mystical attitude in its formulations. . . .[2]

Dante's ideal of the Emperor reminds one of both the Byzantine Emperor and the Russian Czar, especially in view of the canonization of the martyred Czar Nicholas. That the Czar took holy communion at his own table shows that he possessed a quasi-priestly function.

That the advent of the Greyhound is prepared for by the martyrdom of people from both sides of the Trojan War [cf. lines 107-108] is the shadow cast by the reconciliation-of-opposites this savior will bring.

---

2. *The Islamic Tradition* (Amity, NY: Amity House, 1988), p 111.

Canto II

In the face of Hell, Dante's courage begins to fail. He remembers the underworld journey of Aeneas as told by Virgil in his AENEID, and the legend of a similar journey made by St. Paul, and feels unworthy to follow them. Virgil then reveals to Dante that he has been sent to help him by Beatrice, acting as an emissary of Divine Grace. His courage returns.

THE TIME IS DUSK. Dante, as he enters the Inferno, is not *trying* to contact the Other World. Only God can tell us when that level of being should be opened. So Dante is wise to beg for help, and to approach with awe.

The entry into the Inferno reverberates with the quality of the Fall of Man, which was a descent from a higher form of corporeality into a more animal-like condition. The fall of man's body to a lower level is presented symbolically in Gen. 3:21: 'Unto Adam also and unto his wife did the Lord make coats of skins, and clothed them.' In the words of Eastern Orthodox Bishop Ignatius Brianchaninov:

> By the fall both the soul and body of man were changed. In the strict sense the fall was for them also a death. That which we see and call death is in essence only the separation of the soul from the body, both of which had already before this been put to death by an eternal death! The infirmities of the body, its subjection to the hostile influence of various substances from the material world, its crudeness—these are a consequence of the fall. By reason of the fall our body entered into the same rank as the bodies of animals; it exists with an animal life, the life of its fallen nature. It serves for the soul as a prison and a tomb.[1]

1. Cited by Fr. Seraphim Rose in *The Soul After Death* (Platina, CA: St. Herman of Alaska Brotherhood, 1993) pp 52–53.

✠

The image of Beatrice now appears, through Virgil's account of how he received his mission to guide Dante through the Inferno. Virgil tells how she was sent to him in Hell by the Virgin, through the mediation of St. Lucy, who is spiritual vision. (Latin *lux, lucis:* 'light'.) She says to Virgil:

> '*God in His mercy so created me*
>   *That misery of yours affects me not,*
>   *Nor any flame assails me of this burning.*
> *A gentle Lady is in Heaven, who grieves*
>   *At this distress through which I must conduct thee,*
>   *So that stern judgment there above be broken.*
> *In her entreaty she called upon Lucia. . . .*' [91–97]

As Beatrice, through St. Lucy, is a projection of the Virgin to Dante's soul, so once again particular love leads to the universal.

The path to Hell is rugged; it is not the ruggedness of ascent, however, but of contraction. (Jacob Needleman, in *The Heart of Philosophy*, tells a tale of two climbers who meet on a mountain and recount their experiences, which are nearly identical. There is one important difference between them, however: the one is ascending, the other going down.) And what does it mean that although the paw of Hell cannot touch Beatrice, she still weeps? The sorrow of Hell goes through her soul without disrupting it; it is a mysterious thing that the Lady of Heaven can weep.

Dante, on the other hand, has to undergo 'the battle . . . of pity' [4–5]. What Dante must see in Hell could rupture his soul; this is why Beatrice is the right protector for him. She is both the soul itself and the Virtue which refines it. Beatrice, who is Dante's soul, *flees* his harm; she does not combat it [cf. 109–111].

The Virgin in Paradise, speaking to Beatrice, shows her great compassion for Dante:

> '*Dost thou not hear the anguish of his cry?*
>   *Dost thou not see the death that fights against him*
>   *On a river that even the ocean cannot shame?*' [106–108]

That 'river even the ocean cannot shame' is the river of manifestation, which is always involved in instability. Dante's love for Beatrice
is spiritual to the degree that it can set him apart from the dissipation of that river. If we give ourselves completely over to manifestation, we are giving our souls to the river that leads to Hell.
Manifestation, however, while moving in a centrifugal direction,
can nonetheless reflect great nobility on its way. The noble signs visible through manifestation are there to lead us counter to the direction of the manifestation itself, and ultimately carry us back to our
Source in the Unmanifest.[2]

2. Though William Blake, in *Jerusalem* 7:57; 62, says 'pity must join together
those whom wrath has torn in sunder,' he also recognizes the existence of a satanic
pity, hence his declaration that 'pity divides the soul' [*Milton* 8:19]. In *Milton*, the
Fall of Man itself is presented as the result of misguided pity.

Canto III

Virgil and Dante enter the antechamber of Hell, and encounter those souls who pursued neither good nor evil. They reach the river Acheron, where Charon, the infernal boatman, ferries the lost souls into Hell itself. Above the gateway to Hell are the famous words:

Above the gateway to Hell are the famous words:

THROUGH ME THE WAY IS TO THE CITY OF WOE:
    THROUGH ME THE WAY INTO THE ETERNAL PAIN;
    THROUGH ME THE WAY AMONG THE LOST BELOW.
RIGHTEOUSNESS DID MY MAKER ON HIGH CONSTRAIN.
    ME DID DIVINE AUTHORITY UPREAR;
    ME SUPREME WISDOM AND PRIMAL LOVE SUSTAIN.
BEFORE I WAS, NO THINGS CREATED WERE
    SAVE THE ETERNAL, AND I ETERNAL ABIDE.
    RELINQUISH ALL HOPE, YE WHO ENTER HERE.

[Binyon: 1–9]

But how can the power that sustains Hell be Primal Love? Titus Burckhardt, in his essay 'Because Dante is Right', has this to say:

> for Dante, divine love is the origin, pure and simple, of creation: it is the overflowing of the eternal which endows the world, created 'out of nothing', with existence, and thus permits its participation in Divine Being. In so far as the world is different from God, it has as it were its roots in nothingness; it necessarily includes a God-denying element, and the boundless extent of divine love is revealed precisely in the fact that it even permits this denying of God and grants it existence. Thus the existence of the infernal possibilities depends upon divine love, while at the

same time these possibilities are judged through divine justice as the negation that indeed they are.[1]

Though in Hell many are cunning on the purely mental level, like lawyers, without spiritual courage there can be no '*good* of the intellect' [18]. Fear blocks spiritual intuition. And for the damned, fear is not overcome, but is transformed into desire— horribly so:

> '*My son,' the courteous Master said to me,*
>   '*All those who perish in the wrath of God*
>   *Here meet together out of every land;*
> *And ready are they to pass over the river,*
>   *Because celestial Justice spurs them on,*
>   *So that their fear is turned into desire.' [121–126]*

The soul travels quickly to the place of its desire. Everyone assumes that his or her soul would automatically choose Paradise —but in order to desire Paradise, one must possess a soul which resembles it.

The damned in Hell curse everything, reminding one of the constant bickering found in some families: 'God they blasphemed and their own parents/the human race, the place, the time, the seed/Of their engendering and of their birth!' [103–105]. If we are commanded to 'honor father and mother,' it is to teach us not to curse life itself; to do so is to fall into spiritual despair.

Charon is reluctant to let Dante enter Hell [88–89]. This reluctance *sounds* like a painful rejection. How often do we find ourselves rejected by situations because we unknowingly possess qualities that are spiritually higher than the circumstances we confront?

Dante must endure many insults in Hell. Virgil is wise to tell him: Be glad that Charon insulted you. [cf. 127–129]

The souls in this circle, the circle of the whirlwind, are damned because they simply went along with circumstances; they are like dust in the wind. In the words of C.S. Lewis' tempter Screwtape, from *The Screwtape Letters*: 'the safest road to Hell is the gradual one—the gentle slope, soft underfoot, without sudden turnings,

---

1. *Mirror of the Intellect*, pp 94–95.

without milestones, without signposts.' This is the circle of the Cowards who, ironically, are also in another way fearless: they have no fear of God. The Cowards are complacent; their fallen state doesn't seem to bother them. How often does a 'so what?' attitude like this hide a deep, unconscious fear?

Cowardice is also inseparable from envy; they are aspects of each other. The envious soul is opposed to particularity because it cannot accept its own uniqueness. Every uniqueness has an impersonal quality, but one which saves and crystallizes the personal as such. The envious person does not accept his own uniqueness because be balks at admitting this impersonal center to his identity. He fears (wrongly) that it will annihilate all his particular qualities. He fails to see how this impersonal uniqueness is the very thing that will give true form to his personhood. And since he has rejected the impersonal dimension—without, of course, being able to avoid it— it attaches itself to his soul in such a way that it forces him to stereotype others, violating their personhood and placing them in that sort of false hierarchy we call the 'pecking order'.

The cowardly spirits, along with the neutral angels who neither rebelled against God nor remained faithful to Him, are envious of everyone, whether saved or damned. The 'wolf of envy' has them by the throat. In this they are the exact opposite of the souls in the first circle of the *Paradiso*, that of the Moon, who envy no one, even though they occupy the lowest level among the saved.

These souls who simply drifted in this life are now punished in Hell by being driven forward, their unconscious fears revealed:

> *And I, who looked again, beheld a banner,*
> *Which, whirling round, ran on so rapidly,*
> *That of all pause it seemed to me indignant;*
> *And after it there came so long a train*
> *Of people. . . .* [52–56]

> *These miscreants, who never were alive,*
> *Were naked, and were stung exceedingly*
> *By horseflies and by hornets that were there.* [64–66]

The souls of the damned are compared to autumn leaves which fall from the bough:

> *As in the autumn-time the leaves fall off,*
> *First one and then another, till the branch*
> *Unto the earth surrenders all its spoils;*
> *In a similar way the evil seed of Adam*
> *Throw themselves from that shoreline one by one. . . .*
>
> [112–116]

The naked bough, watching them as they fall, is Adam himself. As in life they possessed the human form but did not deserve it, so now, in death, they must shamefully sink before the eyes of it. The true Christian knows that he is fallen, however, and therefore understands the need for prayer and repentance, as well as their efficacy.

Before continuing his journey, Dante requires the certainty that he is not damned—a mercy which comes to him through Virgil's revelation of the meaning of Charon's insult. He needs this certainty because Hell, until one is freed from it, *is* eternal damnation. In the words of Frithjof Schuon, from *Survey of Metaphysics and Esoterism*:

> hell too is a phase of transmigration, in the final analysis [*not* reincarnation, but the passage of the soul through after-death states], but before releasing the soul to other phases or other states it imprisons it 'perpetually', but not 'eternally'; eternity pertains to God alone.... Hell crystallizes a vertical fall; it is 'invincible' because it lasts until the exhaustion of a certain cycle whose duration God alone knows.[2]

Eastern Orthodox theology also allows for the possibility that damnation may not be absolutely eternal, although universal salvation remains a hope, not a dogma. To make a dogma out of it would be to concretize a reality which will not accept such treatment.

The Third Canto ends with earthquake and whirlwind; Dante, seized with 'a bloodred light . . . that conquered all my senses' [134–135] sinks deeper into the Unconscious.

---

2. *Survey of Metaphysics and Esoterism*, p81.

Canto IV

Dante awakens on the other shore of Acheron, on the edge of the abyss. He and Virgil enter Limbo, the First Circle of Hell, where the unbaptized souls of the virtuous pagans dwell, including Virgil himself. Virgil tells Dante the story of Christ's harrowing of Hell, during which He released from Limbo the righteous souls of the Old Testament, and many others. Dante encounters the souls of the classical poets: Homer, Ovid, Horace and Lucan who, along with Virgil and Dante himself, comprise the six greatest poetic intellects. Dante joins their ranks.

The poets travel till they reach a castle with seven concentric walls, surrounded by a flowing stream. Upon entering, they encounter the shades of the classical heroes in a green, flowering meadow, among whom is included Saladin, the Muslim hero who vanquished the Christian crusaders. On a slightly higher level the classical and Muslim philosophers appear, all grouped around the shade of Aristotle.

THE THUNDERCLAP which awakens Dante at the beginning of this Canto is Divine Wrath, with illumination (lightning) implicit within it: 'I started up like one awakened by force' [3].

The souls Dante meets in Limbo are not suffering like those in the ante-Inferno. They are better than all others in Hell because they alone understand what spiritual loss really is. Here is encountered the *essence* of the mystery of who is saved and who is not; that Christ died for those who lived before Him is an expression of this mystery.

Virgil says to Dante, 'Let us descend now into that blind world' [13]. In this particular circle of 'the blind world', however, the inmates are conscious of their blindness. Their condition reminds us of Thomas Merton's description of his father, from *The Seven Storey Mountain,* as one whose artistic sensibilities raised him above the level of society without redeeming him from it. The same is true of so much pagan classical literature, where life remains under the power of the Fates. A Christian looks at this spiritual condition and immediately sees how it needs the incarnation of Christ.

The poets, heroes and philosophers in the circle of Limbo are truly noble; clearly more is going on here than what the orthodox Catholic doctrine of Limbo allows for. But how, we must ask, can the noble be damned? Such damnation is possible because salvation is on a divine scale, and is involved with more than what is merely personal.

This refutes the doctrine of certain psychologists, like Eric Fromm, who confuse social and psychological balance with spiritual salvation. In the words of Martin Lings,

> According to an ancient and still recognized legal principle an accused man cannot plead, in his defense, ignorance of the law; and since in the older civilizations the temporal and the spiritual were organically connected, this principle may well have originated as a prolongation of the dogma that on the Day of Judgement it will not be possible to plead ignorance of the basic truths of religion.[1]

If ignorance of the law is no excuse, then salvation must be by grace, not law:

> *'... I was a novice in this state* [says Virgil]
> *When I saw come this way a Mighty One,*
> *Wearing the crown of victory on his head.*
> *He led forth from here the shade of our First Parent,*
> *And that of his son Abel, and of Noah,*
> *Of Moses the lawgiver, and the obedient*
> *Abraham, patriarch, and David, king,*
> *Israel with his father and his children,*
> *And Rachel, for whose sake he did so much. . . .'* [52–61]

---

1. *The Eleventh Hour: The Spiritual Crisis of the World in the Light of Tradition and Prophesy* (Cambridge: Quinta Essentia, 1987), p1.

The power of Christ to liberate souls from Hell itself is the basis of the Eastern Orthodox practice of praying for the damned, which in Catholicism is strictly prohibited. Dante's position on this question is here shown to be closer to the Greek east than the Latin west.[2]

When Dante asks Virgil, 'and who are these, who've kept such dignity / It sets them apart in manner from the rest?' [74–75], he answers:

> '. . . *The honorable name,*
>   *which echoes up above within* YOUR *life,*
>   *Wins grace in Heaven, and that advances them.*' [76–78]

This gives the *admirer* an unexpected authority, a power which, in worldly terms, is usually ascribed only to the admired. This authority comes from his positive relationship to the Spirit. Dante relates *actively* to spiritual Reality, unlike the souls in Limbo, whose relationship is only passive. Thus he can give them a nourishment essential for their souls' advancement—the prayers of a living man. That their 'name . . . echoes up above within your life' is an image of what it means for an objective ontological hierarchy to be established within one's soul.

Titus Burckhardt, in 'Because Dante is Right', deals with the apparent paradox of souls who are noble, though in Hell:

> To the modern reader, it seems strange that Virgil, the wise and good, who was able to lead Dante to the summit of the Mount of Purgatory, should have to reside like all the other sages and noble heroes of antiquity in limbo, and ante-chamber of hell. But Dante could not transfer the unbaptized Virgil into any of the Heavens attainable through grace. If, however, we look as little more closely, we become aware of a remarkable rift in Dante's

---

2. The Orthodox Christians, somewhat like the Muslims, leave open the possibility that Hell, though it must remain in existence as the manifestation of Divine wrath, may some day be emptied of its inhabitants. Dante apparently embraces this possibility, since he makes no formal distinction between the Hades of the righteous souls who died before Christ and the Hell of the damned—unless the Limbo of CANTO IV is his version of Hades, or one aspect of it.

work, which seems to hint at a dimension that was not developed further: in general, limbo is described as a gloomy place, without light and without sky, but as soon as Dante, together with Virgil, has entered the 'noble castle' where the sages of old walk upon 'emerald lawns', he speaks of an 'open, luminous and high place' (*Inferno*, IV, 115 ff), as though he no longer found himself in the underworld covered by the earth. Men are 'of slow and deep gaze, of great dignity in their behavior, and speak seldom, with mild voices' (ibid., 112–114).[3]

This dimension no longer has anything to do with hell, but neither does it lie directly within the range of Christian grace. In this connection, the question arises: why did Dante not adopt an exclusively negative attitude towards the non-Christian religions? In a passage in the *Paradiso*, where he numbers the Trojan prince Ripheus among the elect, he speaks of the unfathomable nature of divine grace and warns us not to be precipitate in our judgments [Canto xx, 67ff]. What could Ripheus be for Dante other than a distant example of an extra-ecclesiastical saint? We do not say 'extra-Christian', because for Dante every revelation of God, in man, *is* Christ. If Christ died for those who came before him, then Christ's advent is not strictly limited to the world of time. In the words of Justin Martyr:

Christ is the first born of God, his Logos, in whom all people share. That is what we have learned and what we bear witness to. . . . All who have lived in accordance with the Logos are Christians, even if they have been reckoned atheists, as amongst the Greeks, Socrates, Heraclitus and the like.[4]

St. Irenaeus of Lyons taught the same doctrine:

There is only one and the same God the Father, and his Word has been present in humanity from all time, although by diverse dispositions and manifold operations he has from the beginning

---

3. *Mirror of the Intellect*, p 95.

4. *Apology*, I, 46 (PG 6,397), quoted in Olivier Clément, *The Roots of Christian Mysticism* (NY and London: New City Press, 1995), p 296.

been saving those who are saved, that is, those who love God and follow his word, each in his own age.[5]

Christ did not only come for those who, since the time of the Emperor Tiberius, have believed in him, nor has the Father exercised his providence only in favor of people now living, but in favor of all without exception, right from the beginning, who have feared God and loved him and practiced justice and kindness toward their neighbors and desired to see Christ and hear his voice, in accordance with their abilities and the age in which they were living.[6]

And therefore 'he descended into the lower parts of the earth' (*Ephesians* 4:9), the infernal regions, to take to all the dead the good news of his coming, for he is the remission of sins for those who believe in him.[7]

Origen, too, concurs:

There has never been a time when the saints did not have the gift of a spiritual salvation pointed toward Christ. The Word became man at the final hour; he became Jesus Christ. But before this visible coming in the flesh, he was already, without being man, mediator for humanity.[8]

Since Dante is so precise in the *Commedia* on who is saved and who damned, he must also present examples of those who might be saved and might be damned—otherwise his system would remain closed, and would thus deny a certain aspect of God, that of the Divine All-possibility. William Anderson, in *Dante the Maker*, asks: did Virgil have to return to Limbo after guiding Dante, or did he ultimately reach the Earthly Paradise? Dante himself leaves this question open.

---

5. *Against Heresies*, IV, 28, 2 (SC 100 bis, p758), quoted in Clément, *The Roots of Christian Mysticism*, p63.

6. Ibid., IV, 22, 2 (SC 100 bis, p688).

7. Ibid., IV, 27, 2, (SC 100 bis, p738).

8. *Commentary on John's Gospel*, 20:12 (GCS 4, 342), and a fragment of the *Epistle to the Colossians* (PG 14,1297).

It is as if the castle with seven concentric walls, enclosing a garden, were an image of the Purgatorio *within* the Inferno, implying that an alternative way of purgation is available. The fact that Christ could release the souls of many of the non-Christian inhabitants of Hell shows that this hidden way remains mysteriously open. Saladin, for example, though historically an enemy of the Christians before and during the Third Crusade, is nonetheless among those implicitly redeemed [129].[9] Redemption is not, however, merely a subjective state. When Dante addresses Virgil as 'you who honor art and science both,' [73] he is indicating the whole spectrum of knowledge, both emotional and intellectual, both subjective and objective. Salvation is the conformity of our subjective selves to objective Reality.

9. In *Purgatorio* XX:91–96, Dante excoriates Philip the Fair of France as the 'new Pilate' for his persecution of the Knights Templars. And his guide through the upper reaches of the *Paradiso* is St. Bernard of Clairvaux, patron of the Templars, who provided them with a revised rule. René Guénon sees the Templars as keepers of the 'Primordial Tradition', and their occupation of the Temple Mount as symbolic of their position as 'guardians of the Holy Land'—the 'Holy Land' in this case representing the Primordial Tradition itself, given that Jerusalem is a site of central importance to Judaism, Christianity and Islam, the three Abrahamic faiths [see René Guénon, 'The Guardians of the Holy Land', in *Symbols of Sacred Science* (Hillsdale, NY: Sophia Perennis, 2004), pp79–88. He even sees the word *contemplante*, applied to St. Bernard in Canto XXI, line 1 of the *Paradiso*, as concealing the word *temple* (*The Esoterism of Dante* [Hillsdale, NY: Sophia Perennis, 2004, p5, n1]).

Though the Templars fought against Saladin in the Third Crusade, a slanderous story was circulated at their trial in 1308 that they had actually done homage to him while in the Holy Land (Peter Partner, *The Knights Templar and Their Myth* [Rochester: Destiny Books, 1987], p75). Such a story, though unreliable as history, would have been useless as slander if it had not referred to some legend already adhering to the Order of the Temple, in the absence of which it would have sounded patently absurd.

Furthermore, the Arab chronicler Usama ibn Munqidh, who calls the Templars his 'friends', tells of how they allowed Muslims to pray in the al-Aqsa Masjid on the Temple Mount, which was under their control. He recounts the story of one occasion on which the Templars protected some of the Muslim faithful from interruption by Frankish 'newcomers', who did not understand that Muslims do not habitually pray facing toward the east, but rather in the direction of Mecca (Edward Burman, *The Templars, Knights of God* [Rochester: Destiny Books, 1986], p76).

Canto V

Here Dante descends into the Second Circle, the true beginning of Hell, where the souls of the lustful are guarded by Minos, judge of the underworld in the AENEID, *who in life had been King of Crete. The lustful are blown around the Second Circle forever by stormy winds; among them Virgil points out the famous lovers Francesca da Rimini and her husband's brother, Paolo Malatesta.*

PAOLO AND FRANCESCA fell into their adulterous affair after reading, in a French romance, the story of the adultery of Lancelot and Guinevere. Francesca tells Dante:

> 'Love, that on gentle heart doth swiftly seize,
>   Seized this man because of that fair body
>   Taken from me; how it was done still wounds.
> Love, that exempts no beloved one from loving,
>   Seized me with pleasure of this man so strongly,
>   That, as you see, it does not desert me yet;
> Love has led us both unto one death.' [100–106]

Dante holds the romantic poets responsible for delving into deep psychic material without seeing its spiritual implications, which would have allowed them to raise it to a higher level. Dante himself is the complete fulfillment of that romantic tradition, and also its harshest critic; he knows better than anyone how romantic glamour can lead to the loss of eternal life.

Lust blinds reason. In our culture we almost consider this blinding to be legitimate because we see reason as a tyrant, whereas in Thomistic theology reason (*ratio*) is one of the fruits of Intellect (*Intellectus*, the direct intuition of spiritual Truth), and also its servant.

These souls are not deluded, like some in the deeper circles of Hell. They know why they are damned. The *wind* in which the souls of the lustful are blown represents obsessed imagination, in particular sexual fantasy; they are dominated by the demonic Powers of the Air. Wind is also a symbol of the Spirit, but since the damned have turned against the Spirit, they experience it as turning against them. Both the saved and the damned encounter the love of God, but in radically different ways.

The theme of death in love is a common symbol, in mystical poetry, for the union of the soul with God. As Shakespeare says in his poem 'The Phoenix and the Turtle',

> *So they loved, as love in twain*
> *Had the essence but in one;*
> *Two distincts, division none:*
> *Number there in love was slain.*

When Francesca says 'Love has led us both unto one death,' this points to a satanic parody of that Divine Love which transcends all duality.

☩

The figure of Minos, gatekeeper of the Second Circle, appears wrapped in his own tail:

> *There standeth Minos horribly, and snarls;*
> *Examining the sins of all who enter;*
> *He judges and assigns as twists his tail.*
> *I say, that when the spirit evil-born*
> *Cometh before him, wholly it confesses;*
> *And then this connoisseur of every sin*
> *Sees what place in Hell is most right for it;*
> *He wraps himself with his tail as many times*
> *As levels he wishes that soul to be sent down.* [4–12]

The *tail* represents enslavement by the lower self. To submit to the

Will of God is liberation; to rebel against Him is to place oneself in bondage to sin.

The tail is also *time;* the winding of the tail represents temporal cycles.[1] Those in the lower circles are more bound to time than those above. Time weighs heavily in Hell; it always pushes one on; there is never enough time. Simultaneously a terrible tedium is experienced; there is *too much* time; time is always wasted. And it is not only time that changes; the whole *quality of space* (not its quantity) becomes more constricted as one descends the infernal cone.

1. Dante's image of Minos reminds one of the figure of Zervan Akarana, 'Boundless Time', the central mystery of the cult of Mithras, who is pictured as a four-winged, lion-headed man with a serpent wrapped, in spiral fashion, six times around his body, like the tail of Minos.

Canto VI

After fainting, Dante again revives. He is now in the Third Circle, the circle of the Gluttons, who are guarded by Cerberus, the three-headed dog of Hell. They are pounded by a cold and filthy rain. Ciacco appears and prophesies about the future of Florence and the Black and White Guelphs, the latter being Dante's faction. Virgil reveals to Dante the state of the damned after the Resurrection.

THE PUNISHING RAIN is a parody of real mercy. The gluttons, unlike the blest, experience God's mercy and grace as dirty kitchen water; they reject mercy because are disgusted by it.

The souls who are expiating the sin of gluttony in Purgatory experience hunger, not disgust; their appetites are more normal. In Hell, however—as in life—gluttony distorts the human form:

> We walked across those shadows upon whom
> The heavy rain-storm beats, and placed our feet
> On vanities that only seemed like persons. [34–36]
> [See note 3, p163]

Gluttony, as a perversion of a natural instinct, is an attempt to become complete, to fill an empty place in one's soul. The blest can accept fulfillment; for them it is completion. But for the damned the quality of fulfillment, which is based on a spiritual ascent they cannot accomplish, only intensifies their peculiar distortions. And since gluttony, of all the cardinal sins, most distorts the human form, Dante chooses the Second Circle as the place and time of this question to Virgil:

> '. . . Master, these torments here,
> Will they increase after the mighty sentence,
> Or lessen, or be just as strong as now?' [103–105]

In other words, will the sufferings of the damned be greater or less after the resurrection of the body? Virgil answers him:

> '*. . . Return unto thy science,*
> *Which declares, that as the thing more perfect is,*
> *The more it feels of pleasure or of pain.*
> *Notwithstanding that this accursèd people*
> *To true perfection never can attain,*
> *More perfect then than now they are sure to be.*' [106–111]

In the case of gluttony, the soul at the resurrection can expect to be reunited with a gross, distorted body. This is why it can be better understood in the Second Circle than anywhere else how the resurrection of the body can only be a negative thing for the damned.

☦

To stop the hellish howling of Cerberus, Virgil throws dirt into his three mouths:

> *When Cerberus perceived us, the great worm!*
> *His mouths he opened, and displayed his tusks;*
> *Not a limb had he that was not moving.*
> *And my Conductor, with both hands open wide,*
> *Took of the earth, and with his fists well filled,*
> *He threw it into those rapacious gullets.*
> *Just like a dog, who barking while he craves,*
> *Grows quite as soon as he has food to gnaw,*
> *For only to devour food he thinks and struggles,*
> *Likewise became those muzzles filth-begrimed*
> *Of Cerberus the demon, who so thunders*
> *Above those souls, they wish that they were deaf.* [22–33]

Everything is becoming grosser and more materialistic—and implicit in this materialism is *imperialism*: to eat dirt is also to devour land. Gluttony implies the existence of a power complex, a hunger to incorporate everything in one's surroundings: 'dog eat dog'. This is why Ciacco appears at precisely this point, and gives his prophesy relating to the future struggles of Florentine politics. Eating the enemy, becoming fat on him, is not the accumulation of possessions (avarice), so much as an attempt to incorporate the very soul of another, as in C.S. Lewis' image of Hell from *The Screwtape Letters*: 'We [i.e., the devils] want cattle who can finally become food; He [the Almighty] wants servants who can finally become sons.'

'Envy and Pride and Avarice,' says Ciacco, 'Are the three sparks that have set all hearts aflame.' [74–75] These three sins are like an analysis of the sin of gluttony. All have an essentially expansive quality; they force the ego to inflate beyond its true limits. Gluttony is a physical manifestation of this same false expansion.

Canto VII

In the Fourth Circle, Dante and Virgil encounter Plutus, the god of wealth. Here are the Misers and Spendthrifts, who roll heavy weights in opposite directions, run into each other, quarrel, retreat, and then run into each other again on the opposite side of the circle. Virgil explains to Dante the meaning of Fortune.

Descending into the Fifth Circle, where the Wrathful and the Sullen are punished, Virgil and Dante come upon a stream of falling water, which feeds the marsh of Styx below. They arrive at the foot of a tower.

> *'Pape Satan, Pape Satan, Aleppe!'*
> *Thus Plutus with his clucking voice began. . . .* [1–2]

PLUTUS, when he sees Virgil and Dante approach, calls upon Satan; here the conscious worship of the satanic principle begins. Virgil addresses Plutus as 'cursed wolf'—the wolf of avarice in another form.

The sinners on the left are tonsured; they are all members of the clergy. These clerics in the *Commedia* are like our early modern image of bankers, perhaps as portrayed by Charles Dickens in his figure of Ebenezer Scrooge; their service to greed is like as ironic, twisted asceticism.

> *Just as the waves that break around Charybdis*
> *Break upon each other when they meet,*
> *In similar round-dance must these spirits step.* [22–24]

The motion of the lost souls is compared to the clashing waves of

Charybdis, the whirlpool. This represents a dispersion so extensive that it forms its own false center.[1]

Both avaricious Misers and prodigal Spendthrifts are attached to wealth; both have rebelled against Providence, here symbolized by Fortune. Both have forgotten that, in reality, no-one owns anything; as it says in the Koran, only God is the Rich. And both the Avaricious and the Prodigal have so radically lost any sense of proportion that no real individuals remain among them; in Virgil's words, 'The undiscerning life that polluted them/Here makes them muddy, unrecognizable.' [53–54]

Dante now asks Virgil to explain to him what Fortune is. He replies:

> 'He whose omniscience everything transcends
>   Created the heavens, and established who
>   should guide them,
>   That every part may shine to every other
> Distributing the light in equal measure;
>   Likewise in the case of worldly splendors
>   He ordained a general minister and guide,
> That she might move at times the empty treasures
>   From race to race, from one blood to another,
>   Beyond resistance of all human cunning.
> Therefore one people triumphs, and another
>   Languishes, in accordance with her judgment,
>   Which hidden is, as in the grass a serpent.
> Your knowledge has no way to stand against her;
>   She makes provision, judges, and pursues
>   Her governance, as the other gods do theirs.
> The changes that she brings allow no rest
>   Necessity lends her ministry such swiftness
>   That human beings must often change their state.

1. The Buddhist term for manifest existence viewed as the product of ignorance and craving—which, to the enlightened, is inseparable in essence from Nirvana—is *sangsara* or *samsara*, which literally means 'whirlpool': a vortex spinning around an empty center which drags people to their destruction.

> *And this is she who so often is maligned*
> > *Even by those who ought to give her praise,*
> > *Slandering and blaming her without just cause.*
> *But she is joyful and regards it not;*
> > *Happy among the other primal creatures*
> > *She turns her sphere, and glories in her bliss.'* [73–96]

Fortune is a manifestation of the Divine impartiality that must seem partial in this world. Fortune's impartiality renders her stable in the higher realm, but unstable and capricious—though only apparently so—in the lower one. Fortune is transformative; she allots not according to worldly ideas of justice, based on reward and punishment for deeds, but according to spiritual tests and trials, which are expressions of a higher justice. God may test us through deception, or even punish us by means of apparent good fortune. She also prevents situations, and egos as well, from solidifying.

In line 89, 'necessity' refers both to Aristotle's *necessary Being*—a name or epithet of God—and its shadow in this world, the 'whip of necessity'.

✠

Deeper in the Fourth Circle, the souls of the angry, mired in the swamp of Styx, attack each other forever.

> *They smote each other not alone with hands,*
> > *But with the head and with the breast and feet,*
> > *Tearing each other piecemeal with their teeth.* [112–114]

The higher archetype of anger is Justice [cf. 19], the balancing force, as in Thomas Aquinas' doctrine of righteous anger, or the Platonic and Patristic concept of the 'incensive' power of the soul, the legitimate use of which is to repel demonic attack. Anger is that which allows us to take an aggressive stand, but it always needs to be tempered by service to something higher than itself.

The sinners in this circle have been overcome by an anger which has tried to stand alone, cut off from its archetype. This anger sinks back into itself and draws their souls into a horrible stagnation; what could be more terrifying to the imagination than anger become immobile? In effect, such anger *is* a swamp.

But why has Dante placed both the Angry and the Avaricious-and-Prodigal in the same circle of Hell? Clearly the Avaricious and the Prodigal are angry at each other; both claim to have Justice on their side. By placing them in the same circle as the Angry, Dante is showing us how the sin of Avarice makes idols of Anger, of Fortune, and of Justice. To cry out against Fortune while demanding Justice is a contradiction; in doing so, one turns away from God's Will and toward self-will: and this is the essence of Anger.

Canto VIII

Dante and Virgil are still in the Fifth Circle, among the Angry and the Sullen. They see two small flames at the top of a watchtower, a signal to Phlegyas, who arrives in his boat to ferry them across the Styx. Philippo Argenti grabs onto the boat; Virgil pushes him away, after which he is attacked and dismembered by his fellow sinners; Dante is glad. They approach the city of Dis, or Lucifer, where the more serious sins are punished. The devils try to block their way.

THE INFERNAL WATCHTOWER is an inverted sense of spiritual guidance. The boatman Phlegyas[1] gloats over Dante, believing him to be lost: 'Now you are caught, foul soul!' [18] The very demons who draw souls into Hell scorn them for being there; the demon Phlegyas feels a sense of personal insult when he discovers that Dante is not damned.

But Dante also gloats—over the damnation of Philippo Argenti— and Virgil approves:

> '. . . *In weeping and wailing*
> *Long may you stay here, accurséd spirit*
> *For thee I know, though thou art all defiled.'* [37–39]

> . . . *Disdainful soul,*
> *Blessed be she who bore thee in her womb!* [44–45]

What, then, is the difference between Phlegyas' demonic scorn and Dante's glee at Philippo Argenti's damnation? Dante's anger is not essentially demonic because it liberates his soul from the Hell he is

---

1. King of the Lapithae, a son of Mars by Chryse. After Apollo raped his daughter Coronis, Phlegyas set fire to Apollo's temple in revenge.

passing through. It is not the sin of Pride, which he encounters in his own soul in Purgatory, but rather righteous anger; by this anger, Dante praises God in the divine forms of Justice and Wrath.

The salvation of the soul is not a public thing; it is a personal one. Dante is here experiencing a personal liberation through righteous anger. Argenti, the Black Guelph, triumphed in the public realm, but remains damned in the personal one. Here Dante demonstrates how personal feelings are closer to matters of salvation and damnation than public sentiments are; seen in their real forms, they are actually more objective. Dante manifests a faith in Divine Justice which transcends visible circumstances, and is thereby freed from a sense of personal grievance.

☩

Dante and Virgil now become separated from each other; the fallen angels alienate Dante from spiritual guidance. This is a threshold crisis; the threshold is that between the sins related to the passions, and the deeper sins based upon the direct denial of God.

The fallen angels at the City of Dis threaten to detain Virgil, leaving Dante no guide *back* through the circles of Hell to the earth's surface. This is the point of no return. After this point Dante, as a Christian, follows the way of Christ in His harrowing of Hell.

About the demons who have blocked their way, Virgil says:

> 'This arrogance of theirs is nothing new;
>   They used it once before at a gate less hidden,
>   Which still today is missing lock and bolt.
> Above it you beheld the deadly inscription;
>   And now, already past it, one descends
>   Passing through the circles, all alone—
> He by whom this land will be unlocked.' [124–130]

'He by whom this land will be unlocked' is the angel who appears in the next Canto; by implication, however, it is Christ, who opened the gates of Limbo, on which is inscribed 'the fatal text' [CANTO III].

Christ drives the point-of-no-return even deeper. Before the Crucifixion and Resurrection, it was above the level of the Inferno; after
the harrowing of Hell, it was at the point of Limbo; now, by implication, it is at the Fifth Circle. (The earthquake which happened at
the moment of the Crucifixion, and which opened the way into the
Seventh Circle, as recounted in CANTO XII, has a similar meaning.)

To say that Christ died for those who lived before Him—for those
he liberated from spiritual darkness in his harrowing of Hell—is to
imply that the change in the collective psyche Christ brought about
does not entirely depend even upon a conscious knowledge of Him;
it is truly objective.

'The Light shineth in the darkness and the darkness comprehended it not.' [John 1:5] When Christ harrowed Hell, he embodied
completely the Light which shineth in the darkness, and the darkness, which is Hell, did not comprehend him—that is, it did not
understand him. If it *had* understood, Christ would have annihi-
lated Hell in that moment.

Canto IX

Dante and Virgil, before the gate of Dis, are still blocked by the demons. The three Furies appear on the rampart of the city; they threaten to summon the Gorgon Medusa, who turns anyone who sees her into stone; Virgil warns Dante not to look. Then the angel whom they have been waiting for appears. He disperses the demons and opens the gate of Dis. Virgil and Dante enter; they reach the Sixth Circle, where the Heretics are punished inside burning sepulchres.

DIVINE INTERVENTION is difficult in Hell, but it comes when it must. This is the point of greatest fear; Virgil himself begins to wonder whether the promised angel will ever arrive. The two are afraid that they will be able to go neither backward nor forward. Here, at the point of no return, the lowest circles of Hell are mentioned for the first time; within these circles lies the deepest center of despair, of the fear that no return is possible.

At this fear-threshold, Dante asks Virgil whether anyone from Limbo, where Virgil's station is, ever descends this far. He answers:

> 'Seldom it comes to pass that one of us
>   Maketh the journey upon which I go.
> True is it, once before I here below
>   Was called upon by that pitiless Erictho,
>   Who summoned back the shades into their bodies.
> I had not long been naked of flesh, when she
>   Sent me down through all the rings of Hell,
>   To bring a spirit back from the circle of Judas. . . .' [20–27]

Erichtho, the witch, temporarily reunites souls with their bodies for the purpose of *necromancy*—the practice of summoning the spirits of the dead for use in divination, as in the story of King Saul and the Witch of Endor [1 Sam. 28:1–20]. This is the precise satanic counterfeit of the resurrection of the dead.

In this Canto, Dante encounters the Dark Feminine—Erichtho, the Furies, the Medusa—who are the exact opposite of Beatrice. The merciful patronesses, Beatrice, the Virgin and St. Lucy, cannot enter here.

Virgil says to Dante, 'the city of the sorrowing . . . we cannot enter without anger' [32–33]; so righteous anger appears again. Anger can drive one on to the Truth, but not all anger is righteous. What is love in Purgatory or Paradise can only be anger in Hell. To pity the damned is merely a way of hiding from the deeper aspects of love; anger, for all its problems, is closer to true love than this kind of cloying pity.

✠

Now the Furies appear. When Dante sees them, he can no longer hear the voice of Virgil (the voice of wisdom) and this is a great danger [34]. Virgil then covers Dante's eyes so he will not see the Medusa —the sight of whom, according to the Greek myth, turns onlookers into stone.

> 'Turn thyself round, and keep thine eyes close shut,
>   For if the Gorgon appear, and thou shouldst see her,
>   No more returning upward would there be.'
> Thus said the Master; and he turned me round
>   Himself, and thinking my hands insufficient
>   My eyes he shielded with his own as well.
> O ye who still have healthy intellects,
>   Observe the doctrine that conceals itself
>   Beneath the veil of these mysterious verses! [55–63]

Here Dante's 'hands' represent his will, and his 'eyes' his intellect. Dante needs Wisdom, not just will-power, to turn away his gaze from the Medusa—in order to will to divert his attention, in other words, he must *know what to will*—and this same Wisdom also hides *him* from her gaze. In the famous words of Friederich Nietzsche, 'If you gaze for long into the abyss, the abyss also gazes into you.' One of the greatest dangers of the lower psychic forces to a spiritual traveler is that under their influence he may become fascinated and transfixed by the Outer Darkness, the power that leads one always further into the externals of things, where the soul must die. That Erichtho brings the souls of the dead back to their bodies is the dark side of spiritual fascination, called *Avidya-Maya* ('ignorance-apparition') in the Vedanta, which is the exact opposite of Dante's fascination for Beatrice, which is termed *Vidya-Maya* ('wisdom-apparition'). That Virgil places his own hands over Dante's, to shield his eyes, symbolizes the 'Divine ignorance' spoken of by Scotus Eriugena; the existence of illusion must be understood, insofar as the absurdity of evil allows; nonetheless the Divine 'ignorance' of illusion is in reality the highest Wisdom.

Dante is hidden from the Dark Feminine by his spiritual Guide because he needs to reveal something to the reader without the Medusa overhearing what he says. The Medusa is ignorant of the fact that Dante's apparent *descent* into Hell is really a spiritual *ascent*, not a damnation, and Dante is careful not to disturb this ignorance. If the Medusa understood the actual situation, she would repel Virgil and Dante instead of drawing them forward with her power of fascination. Here, by the action of Divine Grace, illusion and self-will—*Avidya-Maya*—are being forced to serve Wisdom—*Vidya-Maya*—both against the Medusa's will and without her knowledge.

The expected angel now arrives, walking across the waters of Styx, and opens the gate of Dis with his wand. As Virgil prevented Dante from looking at the Medusa, so he now directs Dante's attention toward the angel.

The angel is sublime. His passage through the air of Hell creates a great echoing crash,

> *The sound we heard was like that of a wind*
> *That, because it must contend with hotter currents,*
> *Strikes the forest, and, without restraint,*
> *The branches rends, beats down, and bears away;*
> *Proud it goes, great clouds of dust before it....* [67–71]

This great tumult is caused by Hell's resistance to the angelic presence. 'Ah! How full of high disdain he seemed to me!' says Dante.

[88]. The angel speaks:

> *'O banished out of Heaven, people despised!'*
>   *Thus he began upon the horrid threshold;*
>   *'Why do you hold such arrogance within?*
> *Why must you rebel against that Will,*
>   *Which severed from its goal can never be,*
>   *And which has so many times increased your pain?'* [91–96]

> *Then he turned back along the filthy road,*
>   *And spoke no word to us, but had the look*
>   *Of one driven and obsessed by other cares*
> *Than the ones that burden those who stand before him.* [100–3]

The disdain of the angel shows his ontological superiority. This, along with his preoccupation with other (higher) things—'obsessed by other cares'—demonstrates that the demonic level of being is less real than the angelic one. The 'terrible, re-echoing crash' of line 65 is *presumptuousness*, here revealed as opposition to God's will; to oppose that Will is to reject Paradise. The damned can't escape the will of God, and won't obey it.

✠

The Heretics in the Sixth Circle are confined inside burning sepulchres. All heresies must possess fragments of the truth; the fire, here, indicates an attempt to attribute too much reality and significance to a mere fragment, thus generating constriction and heat.

'Those tombs are much more crowded than you believe,' says Virgil; 'Here, like together with like has been entombed' [130–131]. Like-entombed-with-like symbolizes mutual identification, the attempt to base judgments upon an interested group consensus. It is therefore opposed to objective truth, in which such identifications are transcended. In the case of the Heretics, error serves truth by offering itself to be refuted; in the words of Meister Eckhart, 'the more he blasphemes, the more he praises God.'[1]

---

1. As William Blake said in *A Vision of the Last Judgment*, 'to be in Error & to be Cast out is part of Gods Design.'

Canto X

In the circle of the Heretics the travelers encounter the tombs of the Epicureans, among whom is Farinata, leader of the Ghibellines of Florence, who foresees Dante's earthly future. The father of Guido Cavalcanti then appears. He gets the impression, from something Dante says, that his son Guido may no longer be living, demonstrating the truth that although the infernal souls can see the future, they are ignorant of the present.

WALKING among the tombs of the transgressors, Dante asks Virgil,

> 'The people who are lying in these tombs,
>   Might they be seen? already are uplifted
>   All the covers, and no one keepeth guard.' [7–9]
> And he to me: 'They all will be closed up
>   When from Jehosaphat they shall return
>   Here, with the bodies they have left above.
> Their cemetery they have upon this side
>   With Epicurus and his followers,
>   And all who say that soul with body dies. . . .' [10–15]

Epicureanism is inherently complacent; it is a narrow vision of things pursued in the name of safety and security. When the Epicureans denied the immortality of the soul, they gave up their lives to externals; this is why they will not be visible after the general judgment; they will be 'shuttered up'. Their essential vision of things is incomplete, but the General Judgment will nonetheless complete them; it will complete their vision of man's mortality by actualizing it, and so cause them to disappear.

The life of the senses is a tomb. Thus the punishment endured by the Epicureans for their denial of the soul's immortality is to be forced to spend eternity as corpses.

When the soul of Farinata stands up in his tomb and accosts them, Virgil tells Dante, 'Here your words must be appropriate' (literally 'must *count*') [line 39]. Appropriate speech is a way of keeping one's distance from the damned. To speak appropriately to someone is to elicit an appropriate response, one that will reveal that person's true state. This is especially necessary when confronting the Epicureans, the 'civilized damned,' whose sophisticated style can almost make a damned soul look attractive.

Farinata says,

> 'We see, like those who have imperfect sight,
>   The things . . . that distant are from us;
>   This much still shines on us the Sovereign Ruler.
> But when they draw near, or are, our intellect
>   is wholly useless. . . .' [100–104]

To see humanity as only earthly is to deny the human state – and this denial is manifest in Hell by the Epicureans' inability to see the present moment. In the afterlife the Epicureans are 'living out their mortality'. In life they limited themselves to the empirical present, the present simply 'as is,' and denied the Eternal Present. Therefore, in death, they are denied awareness of *any* present moment, because the empirical present is always past.

The Epicureans are ruled by Proserpine, Goddess of the Moon, queen of the underworld [cf. 79–80]. Wisdom, wholeness of perception, symbolized by Beatrice, is implicitly opposed here to the partial perception symbolized by Proserpine, the Goddess of Fate, who rules the material, 'sub-lunary' world. The Moon is also the world of memory, and thus of purely mental knowledge, stored-up knowledge as opposed to direct perception.[1] (According to the folk proverb, all forgotten things go to the Moon; only that which has been forgotten can be remembered. In the words of William Blake, 'memory is eternal death'.) Fate is always predicated on partial knowledge, and this causes fear; Wisdom, on the other hand, reveals the whole form and meaning of one's life *sub specie aeternitatis*.

---

1. The words *moon, mind, measure* and *memory* are etymologically related.

Canto XI

The City of Dis, which the pair have entered, embraces all the lower circles of Hell. Still in the Sixth Circle, the travelers come upon the tomb of Pope Anastasius among the Heretics. Virgil explains to Dante why some sins are more serious than others. Violence is punished in the Seventh Circle. Violence against oneself is worse than violence against others, and worst of all is violence against God. 'Ordinary' fraud is punished in the Eighth Circle, and personal betrayal in the lowest circle, the Ninth.

MALICE IS DIVIDED into sins of *force* and sins of *fraud*. The first is a perversion of the will, the second of the intellect; one is a parody of the Divine Absoluteness, and the other of the Divine Infinity (cf. Frithjof Schuon, *Survey of Metaphysics and Esoterism*).

Virgil and Dante encounter an 'outrageous stench' rising from the abyss. Virgil suggests that they wait until they have become more used to the smell before proceeding. This is a symbol of *reflection*. Reflection generates detachment and builds stamina to face evil—an association not often made, since we believe today that the one who reflects lacks courage, as in the contemporary piece of popular 'wisdom' which commands us to 'just do it'—to which traditional folk wisdom would reply, 'all haste is of the Devil'.

Sinful maliciousness upsets natural justice or balance: 'Of every malice that wins hate in Heaven/Injury is the end. . . .' [22–23]. According to Dante, Pope Athanasius was a follower of Photinus who promulgated the Acacian heresy which denied the divinity of Christ. The sins of incontinence, punished in the circles above, degrade the divinity in man, but do not deny it. Violence and Fraud, punished from here on down, directly deny the Divine/Human center; and this is the essence of injustice.

In Virgil's hierarchy of violence, violence to others is the highest because it is comparatively external. It is less serious than violence to oneself, which cannot help but be more inward, whether we like it or not, and is therefore closer to an attack upon God. To be violent against oneself is to waste the good of life. The final form of this violence is suicidal despair. Kierkegaard, in *Sickness Unto Death*, divides despair into a *despair of necessity* due to the dearth of possibility, and a *despair of possibility* due to an alienation from necessity. Despair of necessity means that the necessities of life grind one down. A person in this kind of despair can follow only one road with no possibility of choosing another, and the burden of it kills that person's spirit. Under the despair of necessity one cannot attain the spiritual depth that would allow one to see into higher dimensions of reality.

Persons in despair of possibility, on the other hand, seem to have more spirit than those in despair of necessity. They believe that a great deal is possible, but do so in an illusory way; they are unable to actualize most of what seems possible to them. Consequently they are often frivolous and cruel in human relationships, since they can't gauge the import of them. Appearances notwithstanding, their despair is therefore no less serious than that of those who are in despair of necessity.[1]

The worst violence is violence against God:

> 'Violence can be done the Deity,
>   In heart denying and blaspheming Him,
>   And by disdaining Nature and her bounty.
> And for this reason doth the smallest ring
>   Seal with its sign both Sodom and Cahors,
>   And whoever speaks from the heart in contempt of God.'
>
> [46–51]

---

1. In alchemical terms, despair of necessity is related to Sulfur, the psychic reflection of the Spirit emanating from the Absolute Reality via Necessary Being, while despair of possibility is related to Quicksilver, the psychic manifestation of the Divine Infinity via Possible Being. When Sulfur and Quicksilver are mutually alienated, both are in despair.

'Cahors' (a French city) represents usury, and Sodom homosexuality. To scorn nature is to scorn God because nature is from God, and is incapable of disobeying Him; this is why Sodomy (apart from the more obvious aspects of domination-and submission it represents) is a form of violence, as in the story in Gen. 19, where the inhabitants of Sodom attempt, unnaturally, to sexually possess the angels of God. Usury too is a violation of nature; unlike the providing of goods and services for just recompense, it is not a natural way to obtain profit. Islamic law, following a similar principle, prohibits the charging of interest on a loan.

Worse than violence is Fraud. Certain kinds of fraud seem almost acceptable to us today—sexual seduction, for example. Lust *per se* is not as evil as lust fulfilled by means of fraud, since this is a form of betrayal, and betrayal is the deepest of all injustices, punished in the final circle of Hell.

Violence is related to the despair of necessity, fraud to the despair of possibility. Fraud is 'man's peculiar vice' [25] because it involves a misuse of the Divine Reality, an attempt by man, created in God's image, to claim for himself divine creative power. To lie is to act as if one had the power to create truth *ex nihilo*, 'out of nothing'. This vice, via the 'cult of creativity,' gets to the heart of the spirit of the Renaissance, where the human attempt to possess Divine power and apply it to worldly endeavors became so virulent that many Christians finally turned against the depth of their own tradition.

In lines 97–111, Virgil gives Aristotle's view of God, Nature and Art:

> *'Philosophy,' he said, 'to him who understands it,*
> *Clearly teaches – and more than in one place—*
> *How Nature follows, in her proper course*
> *From the art of the Divine Intellect itself.*
> *And if you've read your Physics carefully*
> *Not many pages from the start you'll find*
> *That at its best your art must follow Nature*
> *Just as a disciple imitates his master*
> *So your art is the Deity's grandchild, as it were.*
> *From these two principles you'll clearly see—*

If you recall how Genesis begins—
How men should gain their livelihood and advance.
But since the usurer takes another course,
He scorns both Nature and her pupil, art;
He places all his hopes in something else.'

In the trinity of God, Nature and Human Art, Nature and Art are given as those things by which men make their way in life, Nature here being *natura naturans*, the Divine Intellect expressed through Divine Art, as in the biblical story of creation. Usury is sinful because it departs from both Nature and Art, and so participates in Fraud. It does this by pretending to be able to create *good* out of nothing, just as lying claims the power to create *truth*. Usury falsely imitates God, whereas Nature and Art follow the lines set down by God.[2]

This misuse of creativity is the essence of the destructive dynamism of the West.

2. Cf. 'Traditional Economics and Liberation Theology', by Rama Coomaraswamy, *In Quest of the Sacred* (Oakton, VA: Foundation for Traditional Studies, 1994).

Canto XII

Climbing down a steep slope of a rockslide created by the earthquake at the Crucifixion, Dante and Virgil enter the First Ring of the Seventh Circle, where those who were violent against others are immersed in Phlegethon, the river of boiling blood. The Violent are ruled by the Minotaur, and guarded by centaurs, who shoot with arrows those souls who try to emerge farther from the river than their punishment allows. Chiron, their leader, appoints the centaur Nessus to guide the travelers across Phlegethon.

THE ROCKSLIDE shows the inverted dynamism of the Fall; the Violent have fallen under the power of gravity. Violent anger may feel like a kind of expansion, but it ends by turning us to stone.

The Minotaur, the bull-headed giant of the Cretan labyrinth, shows the human form descending to the level of the beasts; the head, the Spirit itself, is now bestial.

> *When he laid eyes on us, he bit himself,*
> *Even as one whom anger racks within.* [14–15]

The Minotaur is anger, and anger can be overcome by being made to 'turn on itself' by *reflection*; anger objectified is anger overcome. When anger is not objectified, when it does not turn on itself in this higher sense, it then blindly attacks itself, and this only aggravates its fury.

In the Christian revelation, God is worshipped as a Person. One of the implications of this is that, since God is the Principle from which we spring ('It is not I who live but Christ lives in me; the Kingdom of Heaven is within you'), in actuality everyone is a real person. Even in Hell people are mysteriously 'all there', though in an uncanny way. The Minotaur and the centaurs, on the other hand, are sub-human *instincts* which are trying to impersonate the human form, in a demonic parody of the Incarnation. They cannot succeed, but in their despairing struggle they can wreak havoc on human souls.

Describing the effects on the Seventh Circle of the earthquake at the Crucifixion, Virgil says,

> '. . . *just a little*
> *Before His coming who the mighty spoil*
> *Carried away from the highest circle of Dis*
> *Upon all sides the deep and loathsome valley*
> *Trembled so, that I thought the Universe*
> *Was thrilled with love, by which there are some who think*
> *The world has often reverted into chaos;*[1]
> *And at that very moment these ancient rocks*
> *Both here and elsewhere tumbled into ruin.'* [37–45]

Here anger is shown as a direct manifestation of twisted love. The denizens of Hell cannot accept the love of God; they can only experience it as chaos.

In the case of the Minotaur, anger takes over the mental faculties directly, this being the symbolic meaning of the bull-headed man. But with the *centaurs,* men with the bodies of horses, the mental faculties are more human, which is why Nessus can temporarily act as guide for Dante and Virgil. But these faculties are totally enslaved to bestiality—not directly overcome by the inhuman, as in the case of the Minotaur, but enslaved by it from below, from the unconscious. They have good native intelligence but are in bondage to their passions; consequently they fall under the power of the Minotaur, the evil genius within the soul whose *conscious* thoughts are demonic— the power that, for example, conceives of evil systems, both philosophical and social. He may have control over his passions (up to a

---

1. According to Allen Mandelbaum, 'In his Metaphysics, Aristotle refers to Empedocles' explanation of the universal order: the principle of Love, which unifies all things, alternates with the principle of Hate, which keeps things discrete and separate. If 'the universe felt love' alone, then all things would fly together by mutual attraction, and the result would be chaos (*The Divine Comedy of Dante Aligheri: The Inferno* [NY: Bantam, 1982], p363, note to lines 41–43).

point), like many who possess power in this world, but his thoughts are essentially evil. This is why, as soon as the Minotaur manifests his anger openly and passionately, he is neutralized; his infernal self-control breaks down.

Dante is in Hell by spiritual necessity, not for pleasure. The damned are there for 'pleasure' in the sense that in life they were attracted to the evils that now torment them. Dante, unlike the damned, is only *passing through;* this demonstrates how necessity, no matter how rigorous, is closer to true freedom than concupiscence is—which, though it gives one a shallow feeling of freedom, in reality is nothing but bondage. But since damnation is also 'necessity,' and necessity is the very thing which will bring Dante through Hell to salvation, could not the implication be that the damned might also be led to salvation? According to the Koran, Hell will last 'as long as the heavens and the earth endure'—yet as the book of *Revelations* predicts, at the end of this cycle, this *aeon*, there will be 'a new heaven and a new earth'. In the words of St. Gregory of Nyssa,

> Perhaps someone, taking his departure from the fact that after three days of distress in darkness the Egyptians did share in the light, might be led to perceive the final restoration [*apocatastasis*] which is expected to take place later in the kingdom of heaven of those who have suffered condemnation in Gehenna.[2]

In lines 118–120, the two travelers encounter the shade of Guy de Montfort, who murdered Prince Henry, Duke of Cornwall, during mass at the Cathedral of Viterbo. According to Mandelstam, the fact that Prince Henry's heart, enclosed within his statue on London Bridge, 'still drips blood upon the Thames,' means that de Montfort's crime remains unavenged. That a situation still exists which 'cries to God for justice' reveals the positive side of anger. The false anger of Hell veils a true anger which is closer to true love. In 'God's bosom' the Divine anger—symbolized by the ever-bleeding heart of Henry—is revealed as God's Majesty, a necessary aspect of the Divine Nature. Both the Kaballah and Jacob Boehme teach the identical doctrine:

2. Gregory of Nyssa, *The Life of Moses* (NY: The Paulist Press, 1978), p73.

that the quality of Judgment, as long as it remains united with the Divine Nature, is good, but as soon as it departs from that Nature and tries to act on its own, it becomes Satanic.

Canto XIII

The travelers arrive on the opposite shore of Phlegethon, the Second Ring of the Seventh Circle, and enter the Wood of the Suicides, where the souls of those violent against themselves have been turned into barren thorn-trees. The souls of the Squanderers then appear, chased by black bitches and torn to pieces.

THE EGO did not create the soul and so the ego cannot destroy it; this is the problem with suicide.

Among the suicides Dante and Virgil meet Pier Della Vigna, the most trusted adviser of Emperor Frederick II, who killed himself because he couldn't endure disgrace. He says:

> 'My spirit, in disdainful exultation,
>   Thinking it could, by dying, escape disdain,
>   Made me unjust against my own just self.' [70–71]

Those who habitually scorn others have, in effect, built their whole lives upon scorn, which is why they can't stand being scorned; they have developed no other psychological or spiritual foundation.

Scorn is intimately related to *jealousy*. 'That courtesan who never from the dwelling/ of Caesar turned away her harlot's eyes/ Who is universal death and the vice of courts/ Inflamed against me every other mind . . .' [64–67] The whore is a type of jealousy, which is also related to suicide in that the victim of jealousy feels that the one he or she is jealous of has stolen (or 'taken') his life; therefore, if he kills himself, it is not really he who is losing his life, but rather the thief who has stolen it.

It is appropriate that the travelers have been guided into the ring of jealousy by the centaur Nessus. In Greek myth this centaur attempted to abduct Hercules' wife Dejanira, but was killed by her husband's arrows. As he lay dying, he instructed Dejanira to collect some of his blood as a love-charm. Later, when Hercules was dallying with Iole, a female captive, Dejanira dipped a robe in the blood of Nessus and presented it to Hercules in an attempt to win him back. However, when Hercules donned the robe, he died in agony: the centaur's blood was poison.

Pier Della Vigna is the sycophant who cannot question his leader, which makes him a symbol of false loyalty. The formal and elaborate speech he uses in the *Commedia*, similar in style to his epistles, is beautiful in a way, but also of a pathetic superficiality. What irony to hear a doomed soul speaking in a mannered, courtly style! 'By the newly-sprouted roots of this strange wood/I swear I never broke faith with that one/Who was my lord, so worth of honor' Della Vigna says [73–75]—but you can't be truly faithful to your lord by betraying yourself. Pier Della Vigna's refined style of expression brings to mind how common the vice of jealousy is in artistic scenes. As William Blake said, in *Auguries of Innocence*, 'The Poison of the Honey bee/ Is the artist's jealousy.'

The Wood of the Suicides, where those who have taken their own lives have been transformed into trees, is ruled by the Harpies, monsters with birds' bodies and the heads of women, their voices an inarticulate screech, their faces pale with hunger. In Virgil's *Aeneid*, the Harpies were appointed by Zeus to torment Phineus, who had been blinded and marooned on a desert island as a punishment for cruelty. Whenever a meal was served to him, it was snatched away and polluted by the Harpies.

That the souls in this circle are menaced by Harpies means that, in an inner sense, they have become Harpies themselves. A soul which is like a Harpy can appear human while functioning on a purely instinctual level, but once the higher faculties are called upon, it is revealed as monstrous: the Harpy is jealousy incarnate. Food in the tale of Phineas represents the giving and receiving of normal affection, as well as normal human speech; in western civilization the 'art of conversation' formed an important part of any communal meal, as in the case of Plato's dialogues. The Harpies are incapable of participating in this give-and-take on the human level. The screeching Harpy is the other side of the silent despair which has driven these souls to suicide. The suicide feels that everyone else can live and act while he is paralyzed; this is the silence which surrounds him and cuts him off from all human contact. If jealousy is based on the feeling that one's life has been stolen, suicide is an attempt to steal life from the Spirit on behalf of the ego, but in neither case can this life really be assimilated: both the harpy and her victim are starving.

That the suicides have been changed into barren trees reminds one of Judas who hanged himself on a thorn tree. The suicides have acted against themselves, in the ultimate perversion of human freedom—so now they are rooted to the spot, as some people who attempt suicide will actually become permanently paralyzed. Trees are an archetypal symbol of life, but the suicide, who has turned against life, now inherits it as a curse.

Pier Della Vigna explains how the souls of suicides are transformed into trees:

> 'When the exasperated soul abandons
>> The body from which it tore itself away,
>> Minos consigns it to the seventh abyss.
> It falls into this forest, and no place
>> Is chosen for it; but wherever Fortune hurls it,
>> There like a grain of spelt it germinates.
> It rises as a sapling, a forest tree;
>> The Harpies, feeding then upon its leaves,
>> Give it pain, but also provide an outlet.
> Like others we shall return to seek our flesh,
>> But none of us may put it on again;
>> It is not just to claim what's been thrown away.
> Here we shall drag our bodies when they rise,
>> And along this dismal Forest they'll be hung
>> Each on the stump of its vindictive shade.' [93–108]

The tree sprouting from the seed of the damned soul is the ego that cannot die. In the words of Titus Burckhardt,

As the ego cannot cast itself into nothingness, it falls as a consequence of its destructive act into the seeming nothingness that the desolate thorn bush represents, but even there it still remains 'I', riveted to itself more than ever in its impotent suffering.[1]

A tree representing an anonymous suicide now calls out to Dante, begging him to collect its severed and bleeding branches, broken by the souls of the Squanderers in their flight through the wood [cf. 139–142]. Of this, Burckhardt says:

> the tree, bereft of its branches, implores the poet to gather the broken branches together at the foot of the trunk, as if the powerless ego imprisoned within still felt itself united with these dead and severed fragments. Here, as in other places in the description of hell, everything in the representation possesses an uncanny sharpness, never in the slightest degree arbitrary.[2]

The soul of the Suicide—and, in another sense, that of the Squanderer—is a victim of self-amputation. He has amputated part of his own life; he has cut off a section of his own time. And yet, ironically, the ego of the Suicide can't let go of anything it has once identified with. The sycophant Della Vigna continues to nurse his grievance forever; he can't cut himself off from his wounded reputation, even in death:

> 'And to the world if one of you return,
>   Let him comfort my memory, which is lying
>   Still prostrate from the blow that envy dealt it.' [76–78]

Now the Squanderers appear, scratched and naked, in flight from a pack of black bitches. Their flight is so violent that they again break branches off the trees in the Wood.

That the Squanderers are pursued and torn by bitches is a symbol of their attempt, through flippancy and shallowness, to rise above their dark feelings. They would like to believe that they are spiritually elevated, exhibiting a godlike carelessness in their squandering of material goods, but this is not so. In reality they are spending all their

---

1. *Mirror of the Intellect*, p 83.
2. Ibid., pp 83–84.

life energy in continually running from their feelings—the bitches which tear at them—and wounding others in the process. They do all they can to make things shallow and meaningless because, like the Suicides, they fear shame and disgrace.

The Squanderers break the limbs of the Suicides because they are fundamentally heartless; they are flippant, nihilistic scorners who respect nothing, who can value nothing. In some ways they are resemble people cursed with a destructive sense of humor; they *fear meaning*, and try their best to avoid it by cultivating flippancy and carelessness. On the other hand, the Suicides 'care' too much, but in the wrong way. To return to Kierkegaard's terminology, the Suicides are in 'despair of necessity,' the Squanderers in 'despair of possibility.'

At the end of the thirteenth Canto, an unnamed Florentine suicide prophesies of Dante's city:

> '*I was of that city who, for the Baptist*
> > *Its original patron [Mars] once chose to reject*
> > *And so always, with his art, he'll make it suffer.*
> > *And were it not that on the pass of Arno*
> > *A few old traces of him can still be seen,*
> *Those citizens, who afterwards rebuilt it*
> > *Upon the ashes left there by Attila—*
> > *All their labor would have been in vain.*' [143–150]

The first patron of Florence is Mars, who stirs up war and civil strife. John the Baptist represents a higher form of anger than Mars; he is the patron of spiritual (unseen) warfare: as he says in the Gospel of Matthew, 'Even now the ax is laid to the root of the trees; every tree therefore that does not bear good fruit is cut down and thrown into the fire.' [Matt. 3:10] The war against the passions is also a form of civil (internal) strife.

John the Baptist is a higher octave of Mars just as—in Muslim terms—the 'greater *jihad*' against the passions is a higher form of the 'lesser *jihad*' against an outer, material enemy. The greater *jihad* takes precedence, but the need for the lesser never permanently disappears; it, too, has a constructive as well as a destructive side. Mars, in his positive aspect, allows the city to be rebuilt: 'Unless the Lord build the house, they labor in vain who build it.' Aggression can be positive, but suicide is its most negative use; Pier Della Vigna's suicide was really an act of aggression against others, though directed against himself.

Canto XIV

In the Third Ring of the Seventh Circle, filled with burning sand, Virgil and Dante encounter those violent against God. Some of them lie supine, some sit huddled, and some are never allowed to stop moving: they are the Blasphemers, the Usurers, and the Sodomites. A rain of fire falls on all of them.

Dante sees a giant lying among the supine, cursing God; Virgil tells him that this is Capaneus, one of the Seven Against Thebes. Virgil explains to Dante the origin of Acheron, Styx, Phlegethon and Cocytus, the four rivers of Hell, from the tears of the Old Man of Crete.

THE RAIN OF FIRE which falls on the Violent against God is an inversion of Divine Grace, a kind of negative Pentecost. The curse of the blasphemous falls back on them because they think they *can* effectively curse God; they do not realize that they are included in Him. In the words of Meister Eckhart, 'the more they blaspheme, the more they praise God.' Since they have blasphemed Him, their torment is the only way they can experience being included in Him—and so their very suffering, since it is the dawning of their knowledge of God, is a form of praise.

> *Of naked souls beheld I many herds,*
> > *Who all were weeping very miserably,*
> > *And all of them seemed ruled by different laws.*
> *Supine upon the ground some folk were lying;*
> > *And some were sitting all drawn up together,*
> > *And others went about continually.*
> *Those going round were far more numerous,*
> > *And fewer those who lay down to their torment,*
> > *But those had tongues more loosed to lamentation.* [19–27]

God is One, but there are many ways of blaspheming Him; this variety lies in the partiality of the souls themselves. The souls of the blasphemers only *seem* to be ruled by different decrees. Those who lie flat on the ground have profaned God, dirtied Him. The huddled are those who, in life, fled from Him through dissipation and inflation, and thus became attenuated, externalized. And the restless are those who have belittled God, made light of Him.

> *O'er all the sand-waste, with a gradual fall,*
> > *Were raining down distended flakes of fire.* . . . [28–29]
> *As Alexander, in those torrid parts*
> > *Of India, beheld upon his host*
> > *Flames fall unbroken till they reached the ground.*
> *Wherefore he wisely commanded all his soldiers*
> > *To trample out the flames upon the soil,*
> > *Before new flames were added to the old.* . . . [31–36]

Blasphemy spreads like wildfire. It's easy to become unconscious of one's blasphemy in a profane age like ours, which is why it is necessary to stamp out blasphemous thoughts immediately.

✠

Capaneus is described by Dante as 'Who is he. . . . / Who lies there all lowering and scornful / such that the rains can't seem to soften him?' [46–48]; he says of himself: 'Such as I was in life, I am in death' [51]. He arrogantly and foolishly believes that his defiance of God is somehow successful, and God's wrath impotent: '[If He] shot His bolts at me with all His might / He would not even then have a joyous vengeance' [59–60].

Capaneus sees the one punishing him as Jove; in so doing he projects upon God his own egotism. What Thomas Merton says of Prometheus, in his 'Prometheus: A Meditation', is applicable here, particularly since Capaneus, in his attempt to prove that Jove is not invincible, harks back to the war between the Olympian Gods and the Titans:

The small gods men have made for themselves are jealous fathers, only a little greater than their sons, only a little stronger, only a little wiser. Immortal fathers, afraid of their mortal children, they are unjustly protected by a too fortunate immortality. To fight with them requires at once heroism and despair... since Prometheus [i.e., the titanic principle] cannot conceive of a true victory, his own triumph is to let the vulture devour his liver: he will be a martyr and a victim because the gods he has created represent his own tyrannical demands upon himself.[1]

In lines 103–114, Dante introduces the figure of the Old Man of Crete, presumably a statue, who stands inside of Mount Ida, where Zeus' mother Rhea hid her son from the his devouring father Saturn, his infant cries drowned out by the chants and clashing cymbals of her followers, the Corybantes. The Old Man is apparently modeled on the statue described in Daniel 2:31–35, which symbolizes the doctrine of the four descending world-ages of a given cycle of manifestation—golden, silver, bronze (or brass), and iron—a doctrine which is found in Ovid's *Metamorphoses*, in the Hindu Puranas, and even in the mythology of the Hopis.

> '*A huge old man stands in the mount erect,*
> > *Who holds his shoulders turned towards Damietta,*
> > *And looks at Rome as if it were his mirror.*
> *His head is fashioned of the purest gold,*
> > *And of pure silver are the arms and breast;*
> > *Then he is brass as far down as the fork.*
> *From that point downward all is choicest iron,*
> > *Save that the right foot is made of fired clay,*
> > *And more he stands on that than on the other.*
> *Each part of him, except the gold, is cracked*
> > *And every crack is running with his tears*
> > *Which, gathered together, pierce the cavern's floor.*' [103–114]

The Old Man of Crete is the terrestrial existence of man in his

---

1. *Raids on the Unspeakable*, (NY: New Directions, 1966), pp 83, 85.

degeneracy; he is an image of man's descending path. It's as if his tears were the souls of the damned, more of them in each succeeding age; they are whatever sinks below integral human life and into the state of Hell. Looking west, toward Rome, he sees humanity only as it is dying. His back is to Egypt, the primordial, which in its original essence partakes of the earthly paradise; he cannot see the East, the point of humanity's spiritual birth. West is the direction of outer manifestation and spiritual death; facing west, he stands as a symbol of the decline implicit in manifestation itself.

To rest on the right foot, made of clay, is to rely on what is ontologically higher, even though it is weakest in terms of its earthly manifestation; this may represent, among other things, the position of spiritual religion in the face of political power. In the latter days, the highest, in this world, is seemingly also the most unstable.

The red rivulet of the Old Man's tears appears precisely here, in this Canto, because at the point of blasphemy the human form itself begins to be destroyed: the very definition of the four descending world-ages is the progressive loss of the vision of God, upon which any humanity worth the name is based.

Dante compares the bloody stream, which is Phlegethon, to the sulphurous hot springs of Bulicame, which fed the houses of prostitutes near Viterbo. 'Nothing has yet been witnessed by thine eyes,' says Virgil, 'so notable as this river here before you / Which quenches all the little flames above it' [88–90]. Passion (the fire) turns moist when it nears the prostitutes, here symbolized by bloody Phlegethon; the heat of passion can't burn out the wateriness of sexual manipulation, because the two are intimately related.[2]

'Where's Phlegethon, and where is Lethe?' asks Dante [130–131], and Virgil replies:

> *'In all thy questions truly thou dost please me,'*
> *Replied he; 'and yet the boiling of the red water*

---

2. Here again we see portrayed the barren warfare between the psychic masculine and feminine principles—called, in alchemical terms, Sulfur and Quicksilver— a warfare which can only be brought to a peaceful conclusion by the catalytic action of the Salt of the Earth.

Itself might serve to answer one of them.
Though not inside this ditch, thou shalt see Lethe,
  There where the souls retreat to cleanse themselves,
  When sin repented of is set aside.' [133–138]

Dante here darkly intuits that Lethe, the river of the Earthly Paradise, will purify him of the vision of Phlegethon. This is the barest hint of Purgatory, which here in the Inferno can't be spoken of openly.

Canto XV

Again the Third Ring of the Seventh Circle, the zone of the Sodomites, the 'violent against nature'. Dante meets his mentor Bruno Latini; they greet each other with great affection. Also among the Sodomites are Priscian, Francesco d'Accorso, Andrea dei Mozzi and Pope Boniface VIII.

THE SODOMITE is violent against nature because he denies relatedness to the Other; his erotic energy is turned inward. If he were to open himself to the opposite sex he would encounter the Spirit, but he doesn't want this. The barrenness of the Sodomite is intellectual as well as sexual; he wanders on hot, barren sands.

The figure of Brunetto Latini is an indictment of the secular humanist intellectual. ' . . . in the world from hour to hour [Mandelbaum has 'from time to time'] / You showed me how man becomes eternal. . . .' says Dante [84–85]. How ironic these lines are! Clearly Brunetto had some vision of eternity, but it was marred on the one hand by an excessive attachment to time—thus its intermittent quality—and on the other by an implicit belief that eternity derives from man rather than man from eternity. His writings could help Dante glimpse eternal truths, but they could not help Brunetto save his soul. Nor could they, in themselves, save Dante; his salvation was from another source.

The crucial difference between Dante and Brunetto, both very cultured, talented men, is that Dante can see Beatrice, the Divine Feminine, the symbol of Holy Wisdom. The spiritual Sodomite, on the other hand, will associate with others only so long as they are in some sense his own reflection. Unlike Dante, he refuses the encounter with anyone or anything which might cause him to witness spiritual realities beyond the circle of his ego.

Dante describes the banks of Phlegethon in these terms:

> *Even as the Flemings between Wissant and Bruges,*
> *Fearing the flood that towards them hurls itself,*
> *Build up dykes to put the sea to flight....* [4–6]

And he says of the Sodomites he meets that 'They knit their brows and squinted at us—just as an old tailor at his needle's eye' [20–21]. The *dykes* and the *squint* both indicate a limited perception of spiritual realities. The intellectual Sodomites are intelligent on a certain level, but they remain spiritually blind. Brunetto Latini's intelligence is external to his immortal soul; it cannot affect his *will*.

> *I said, 'with all my strength I beg you, stay*
> *And if you wish me to sit down with you,*
> *I will, if it pleases him with whom I go.'*
> *'O son,' he said, 'whoever of this herd*
> *A moment stops, lies there a hundred years,*
> *Nor can he shield himself when fire strikes.'* [34–39]

This shows the total absence of any contemplative space. It is a prophesy that in the Renaissance, and in Renaissance knowledge, there will be no rest.

> *I did not dare to go down from the road*
> *Level to walk with him; but my head bowed*
> *I held as one who goeth reverently.* [43–45]

Dante as a youth 'looked up' to Brunetto as someone who possessed true cultural knowledge, knowledge not without value because it pertains to things of the soul. But Brunetto was not centered in the salvation of the soul, which means that, even as a student, Dante was on a higher level than he.

> *'. . .If thou thy star do follow* [says Brunetto],
> *Thou canst not fail to gain a glorious port,*
> *If I judged thee right when still in gracious life.*

> *And if I had not died so prematurely,*
>   *Seeing Heaven had been merciful to thee,*
>   *I would have helped sustain thee in thy work.'* [55–60]

Brunetto, however, could not have really helped Dante more than he did; he did not die 'too soon' for Dante, but for himself.

In lines 61–78, Brunetto Latini castigates 'that malicious, ungrateful people' among the Florentines, 'come down, in ancient times, from Fiesole,' and contrasts them with 'the sacred seed of those few Romans who remained....' He prophesies that Dante's fortune holds great honor for him, but warns him that due to this very fame 'one party or the other will be hungry for you—but keep the grass far from the goat.'

The divided heredity of Florence is a symbol of divergent tendencies within the soul. Dante's goodness and love of justice will force him into exile; it will deny him a place in this world. It is precisely here, in the circle of the Sodomites, that Dante must transcend partisanship, because there is something in homoeroticism that has to do with group identification, with the adolescent peer group, the gang. In the words of William Blake,

> *Twas the Greeks love of war*
> *Turnd Love into a Boy*
> *And Woman into a Statue of Stone*
> *And away fled every Joy*

In reply to Brunetto's glowing prediction of his future fame, Dante has this to say:

> *'This much will I have manifest to you:*
>   *Provided that my conscience does not accuse me,*
>   *For whatsoever Fortune I stand ready.*
> *This pledge is nothing novel to my ears;*
>   *So let Fortune turn her wheel as she may please;*
>   *Likewise let the peasant turn his mattock.'* [91–96]

'He's listened well who taketh note of this' Virgil says [99].

When Dante says 'so long as I am not rebuked by conscience, I stand prepared for Fortune,' he differentiates between guilt and misfortune; not every misfortune is a punishment.

Fortune has to do with manifested form. Form cannot be overcome on its own level; it can only be transcended—and the call which has come to Dante to transcend partisanship is one aspect of this. About the mystery of the formless Godhead, Dionysius the Areopagite says: 'It exceedeth all things in a super-essential nature, and is revealed in Its naked truth to those who pass right through the opposition of fair and foul.'[1] Detachment or *apatheia* in the face of good and bad fortune thus represents a step toward the Transcendent Godhead.

In saying 'let Fortune turn her wheel as she may please; likewise let the peasant turn his mattock,' Dante is referring to the mysterious relationship between predestination and spiritual labor. Labor and Fortune are separate on the level of manifestation, but both are part of something greater; in the Formless realm, in the Invisible world, they are united.

---

1. Cited by Whitall Perry in *A Treasury of Traditional Wisdom* (Cambridge: Quinta Essentia, 1991), p979.

Canto XVI

Still the Third Ring of the Seventh Circle, where the travelers meet more Sodomites, including three from Florence: Guido Guerra, Teg-ghiaio Aldobrandi and Jacopo Rusticucci. Dante laments the deca-dence of his city; the travelers again reach the river of Phlegethon; the shadowy form of Geryon rises from its waters.

THE SOULS OF Guido Guerra, Tegghiaio Aldobrandi and Jacopo Rustciucci now accost Dante. It only increases their tragedy for these three still to possess noble characteristics that nonetheless lack the power to save them; not even eternal damnation can alter the fact that man is created in the image and likeness of God. In the words of Gai Eaton,

> We are condemned to totality because no amount of wishful thinking and no amount of theorizing, no sheltering under the earth's weight and no act of self-destruction, can make us less than we are. We can only pretend to be other than viceregal crea-tures with a viceregal responsibility, and this pretense is to be stripped away on the Day of Judgment.[1]

> *When the three shades all together began to run.* . . . [4]
> *Towards us came they, and each one cried out:*
>   *'Stop, thou; for by thy dress thou seemest to us*
>   *To be a native of our indecent city.'* [7–9]
> *Unto their cries my Teacher paused attentive;*
>   *He turned his face towards me, and 'Now wait,'*

1. *King of the Castle: Choice & Responsibility in the Modern World* (Cambridge: Islamic Texts Society, 1990), p 187.

He said; 'to these we should be courteous.' [13–15]
They formed of themselves a wheel, all three of them
As champions stripped and oiled are wont to do,
  Watching for their advantage and their hold,
  Before they come together with thrusts and blows.
Thus, wheeling round, did every one his face
  Keep turned to me, so that in opposed directions
  His neck and feet continually traveled. [21–27]
Then they broke up the wheel, and in their flight
  It seemed as if their agile legs were wings. [86–87]

These three souls are forced by the remnant of good in them to look toward Dante because he is spiritually more exalted than they. These souls, like other triplicities in the *Inferno*, are a parody of the Holy Trinity. In the Trinity, the faces of the three Persons are turned toward each other, and thus simultaneously toward Beyond Being, but here the implication is one of profound disunity. This ontological disjointedness is shown by the fact that their vision has nothing to do with the actions of their bodies, and is even opposed to them. Without Unity they can neither face each other nor see what they themselves are doing, which is why they are continually flying apart. Their actions are automatic.

Sodomy implies the very kind of inner division that the bodies of these three manifest, because life energy is diverted from its natural channels; the wholeness of the soul is broken. 'I', says one of them, 'was Jacopo Rusticucci; certainly, above all else, my savage wife destroyed me' [43–45]. The sodomite would choose, or fate would choose for him, a savage wife, one that would drive him even further into sodomy. His wife is his soul, and thus also his fate—a kind of vicious cycle, like that formed by the three wheeling souls.

They ask Dante, ironically:

'*Say if valor and courtesy still dwell*
  Within our city, as they used to do,
  When we lived there. . . .' [66–68]

And Dante informs them:

'New inhabitants and sudden gains,
   Pride and extravagance have engendered in thee,
   Florence, so that you weep for it already!'
In this way I cried out with face uplifted;
   And those three, taking that for my reply,
   Looked at each other, as one looks at truth. [73–78]

The news that Florence has further degenerated can only increase the torment of these degenerate souls; it cannot purify them. The natural tendency—'supernaturally natural', as Schuon would say— is to expel from one's soul all that one sees as evil. But in the *Inferno* this is impossible. The damned are only further burdened and contaminated by the evil they witness.

Finally, they make this request:

'Therefore, if thou escape from these dark places,
   And come to rebehold the lovely stars. . . .
See that thou speak about us unto men.' [82–83, 85]

As we have already pointed out, the deeper Dante and Virgil descend into the Inferno, the closer they come to the Purgatorio; this is why the damned can now imagine the beauty of the stars, which Dante will not see again until he reaches the foot of Mt. Purgatory—but it is a beauty the damned will never see.

Thus downward from a bank precipitate,
   We heard the roaring of that blackened water,
   So that our ears it soon would have offended.
I had a cord, kept tied around my waist;
   I'd planned to use it, in a former time
   To rope the leopard with the painted hide.
And after this from around me I'd untied
   As my Conductor had commanded me,
   I held it toward him, gathered up and coiled,
Whereat he turned himself towards the right,
   And at a little distance from the edge
   He cast it down into that deep abyss.

'And certainly some new thing must reply,'
  I said within myself, 'to this new signal
    The Master is so following it with his eye.' [103–117]
He said to me: 'Soon there will upward come
  What I await; and what thy thought is dreaming
    Must soon reveal itself unto thy sight.'
Always to that truth which has the face of falsehood,
  A man should close his lips as long as he can,
    Because, though he be blameless, it brings him shame;
But here I can't be still. . . . [121–127]
Athwart that dense and darksome atmosphere
  I saw a figure swimming upward come,
    Amazing even to the firmest heart. [130–132]

The painted leopard represents the *illusion* of lust. For Dante to dream of catching it with the cord around his waist—reminiscent of a monk's cincture—shows that his intent is confused, whether to fulfill lust or bridle it. You can't catch lust and fully live it out on your own terms; neither can you bridle it on its own level. The cord loosed, then handed to Virgil knotted and coiled, shows Dante in the act of allowing his Guide, here a reflection of the spiritual Intellect, to see the knots of lust in his soul, and thereby dominate them. He feels shame at the dawning of the vision of the monstrous figure who will be revealed as Geryon because it is the image of the disorder of his soul externalized, as Tibetan lamas will externalize a *tulpu*, a form created in visualization which is visible to others. The purpose of this dreadful vision is to fully constellate or crystallize the evil in his soul so that it will no longer exercise a subtle, hidden influence. If a man is shamed before the vision he sees, it is because a true vision, every bit as much as a planned or commanded action, implies responsibility. The sins of the souls Dante has met in his journey through Hell are implicit in his own soul, even though he may not have committed those sins in act, but only in thought.

'The truth that seems a lie': In a way Dante's vision of the monster is hallucinatory, less real than the souls he sees around him. But in another way it is more real, since it faces him with a truth he could not have faced otherwise. He must 'close his lips as long as he can,' because to speak of this vision is to accept full responsibility for it, and this must not be done prematurely. Speaking too soon will destroy the speaker, or his hearers, or both—as in the case of decadent, demonic art. However, Dante must speak; his duty is to expose the demonic, not indulge in it.

Canto XVII

Geryon, the Monster of Fraud, appears. The travelers encounter the Usurers, who were violent against both Nature and Art. They mount Geryon's back, and descend to the Eighth Circle.

GERYON'S FUNCTION is to lure souls into the deeper circles of Hell. Above him, the souls of the damned are violent; here they are deluded, and possess the power to delude others.

> *The face was as the face of a just man,*
> *Its semblance outwardly was so benign,*
> *But all his trunk, the body of a serpent.*
> *Two paws it had, hairy unto the armpits;*
> *The back, and breast, and both the sides of it*
> *Were decorated with knots and little circles.*
> *Background or embroidery of greater color*
> *Never in cloth did Turk nor Tartar make,*
> *Nor were such tissues by Arachne spun.*
> *As sometimes boats will lie upon the shore*
> *That are half within the water and half on land;*
> *Or as among the guzzling German, at his post*
> *The beaver plants himself to wage his war;*
> *So that vile monster lay upon the barrier*
> *Made of stone, that keeps away the sand.*
> *His tail was wholly quivering in the void,*
> *Twisting upwards with its poisoned fork;*
> *The tip just like a scorpion's sting appeared.* [10–27]

In Geryon appear three natures: the human (his head), the mammalian (his arms) and the reptilian (his body). All three, however, serve the powers of abysmal delusion; thus Geryon's truest nature is in his lowest part, his reptilian tail, which is ambiguous and deceptive, at once forked, pointed and hooked like that of a scorpion. That his tail is *forked* symbolizes *duplicity*, which is based on hidden contradictions and double meanings. That his tail is *pointed* is a satanic counterfeit of one-pointedness or concentration; attention is contracted rather than centered. And that his tail is the tail of a *scorpion* represents fraud in its essential form: with it he hooks his victims, and then administers the *coup-de-gras*, the poison of illusion.

Geryon's human face is all appearance; his bestial arms, where his evil begins to be revealed, represent a crude emotional warmth which disguises his true reptilian nature. His colorful hair and skin (or clothing) give the appearance of a rich soul, related to the mammalian warmth of the hair which spreads from his arms to his chest and flanks, as if to hide the reptilian body, which is the real determining factor. His face is that of a 'just man'; it inspires confidence, like the guileless personality of the 'confidence man.' His colorful torso symbolizes charm and charisma; the ringlets of his spreading hair, which seem to become transformed into a patterned fabric, remind one of the symbolism of the tress or ringlet in Sufi poetry, denoting the fascinating and enthralling attraction of the Divine Beloved (*Vidya-Maya*), which appears here in inverted form, as Arachne's deadly web (*Avidya-Maya*). And [9] Geryon's tail remains hidden. Trust puts you at your ease; dazzle and glitter hide what you normally would not trust—and then the reptilian tail does its work.

The comparison of Geryon to a beaver here demonstrates how fraud muddies the waters; the fraudulent person does not want clarity of vision, but instinctively destroys it. Those who absolutize the subjective, who proudly and complacently tell us how they hate objectivity, are more involved with fraud than they know.[1]

Geryon is evil, then, because his reptilian nature is central. 'But,' some would say, 'is there not both good and evil in Geryon? After all, he has a just head, and warm, colorful mammalian arms, and (perhaps) a mammalian torso as well.' The answer is: No, because it is the reptilian nature that is operative; head, arms and torso serve the tail; they have no power of their own. So Geryon, symbol of fraud, is the image of an inverted hierarchy; the tail rules in place of the head.

✠

Next, the travelers encounter the Usurers:

> *Sorrow and grief were bursting from their eyes;*
> *This way and that they kept off with their hands*
> *Sometimes the flames, sometimes the burning soil:*
> *Not otherwise will dogs do in the summer—*
> *Now with muzzles, now with scratching paws—*
> *When fleas or gnats or horseflies land and bite them.* [46–51]

The Usurers give a dog-like impression because they've given their entire souls over to greed, which destroys their natural human dignity. The opposition of the medieval aristocracy to the usurious merchant class can thus legitimately symbolize the inner struggle that takes place when the vice of avarice attempts to blot out the soul's natural nobility. (As Meister Eckhart said, 'The soul is an aristocrat.') We can see here why Christian societies once prohibited

---

1. In his poem 'Hymn to St. Geryon, I,' Beat Generation poet Michael McClure does absolutize the subjective, precisely:

> ... Not politics
> but ourselves—is the question.
> HERE I SEE IT WITH FLOWERS ENTERING INTO IT
> that way.
> Not caring except for my greatness, caring
> only for my size I would enter into it.
>
> THE SELF'S FREE HERO
> . . . . .
>
> But I love my body and my face only
> first and not the others'
> . . . .
>
> I am the body, the animal, the poem
> is a gesture of mine.

Here McClure defines a theory of poetics that is the precise opposite of the principle of the *objective correlative* enunciated by T. S. Eliot in his essay 'Tradition and the Individual Talent'.

usury, as Muslim societies still do. (Perhaps these usurious souls are another form of the black bitches who chase the squanderers in Canto XIII; loan sharks certainly do pursue squanderers.)

The Usurer is violent against God because he believes he can magically manufacture value out of nothing, whereas in reality only God is the source of value. To charge interest is thus a sort of satanic parody of God's creation of the universe *ex nihilo*. Karl Marx was right insofar as he knew that value had to be based on something realer than an essentially fraudulent manipulation of finances; he identified this real basis with human labor. But he, too, denied God as the source of all value, forgetting that the power to labor and the material conditions that make labor possible are all freely provided by the Creator.

The purses bearing family crests that are hung around the necks of the Usurers, as if in the place of crosses, are hideous; their bearers are burdened by these objects, yet fascinated by them. These purses satirize their owners, though they seem entirely unaware of the fact.

The monster Geryon is now compelled to carry Dante and Virgil to the next circle. With the pair on his back he must move ponderously and slowly, which is uncharacteristic of him. It is as if he is being forced to reveal his methods to the travelers; and just like any confidence trickster, he hates to have his professional secrets exposed. At first he backs off, because to show his fair face and hide his ugly tail is his usual mode of operation. Then he circles down with a wheeling motion, carrying his passengers, and when he lets them off—as he has dumped so many victims in the past who lacked the spiritual protection of these two—he moves away from them as fast as he can, 'like an arrow from the string' [136], because he loathes the presence of any embodiment of Truth. The suffering of the lower circles of Hell is actually the *result* of the wheeling motion of Fraud, though Dante cannot see or feel this motion until its effects become apparent.

In describing his descent into the Eighth Circle on the back of Geryon, Dante compares his fear to that of Icarus and Phaethon, two early air travelers who lost their lives through flying. Both were burned by the sun, the one by coming too near it, the other by trying to control it. Those involved with Fraud are attempting to directly tap the Spirit to embellish their egos, and so end by being burned—like many false spiritual teachers, such as those we will meet in the next circle. Both Icarus and Phaethon are images of *hubris*. Icarus in particular is the Jungian *puer aeternus* par excellence, the young man who, *because* of his immaturity, can reflect the Spirit while in no way embodying it, thus manifesting far more glamour than someone with a more stable character. Fraud always involves *hubris*—the sin of 'hype'.

Canto XVIII

Next comes the interminable Eighth Circle, called Malebolge or 'evil pouches,' of which there are ten; it is here where 'simple' fraud is punished; its inmates are being scourged by demons. The travelers pass through the First Pouch, that of the Seducers and Panders, and the Second, that of the Flatterers, with Thaïs, symbol of sexual flattery, occupying the lowest place.

While I was going on, mine eyes confronted
　　Someone else. . . . [40–41]
And he, the scourged one, thought to hide himself,
　　By lowering his face, but little help it gave. . . . [46–47]

THE FLATTERERS AND SEDUCERS are beginning to participate directly in the realm of illusion. As in the world they tried to put a false face on their actions, so now, in Hell, this face is removed, which is why they are ashamed before Dante: they have 'lost face'.

The Seducers and the Panders (pimps) imposed their will upon others in life; here they are punished in a similar manner. But their punishment is, in another way, the converse of their sin: as they *led* others astray, so now they are being *driven*. In life they felt they could manipulate others easily; in hell they are harshly pushed: the rude breaking of one will by another—which, in the world, was hidden under a veil of seduction—is here revealed in its true form. And they are also punished by 'eternal circlings'; the Flatterers and Seducers are eternally forced to 'go back' on what they've said. Their glib, easy faithlessness is ultimately unveiled as the seed of a terrible destiny.

And the good Master, without my inquiring,
  Said to me: 'See that tall one who is coming,
  And for his pain seems not to shed a tear;
Still what a royal aspect he retains!
  That Jason is, who by his heart and cunning
  Deprived the men of Colchis of their ram.
He by the isle of Lemnos passed along
  After the daring women, pitiless
  Had unto death devoted all their males.
There with love signs and with ornate phrases
  Did he deceive Hypsipyle, the maiden
  Who first, herself, had all the rest deceived.
There did he leave her pregnant and forlorn;
  Such sin unto such punishment condemns him,
  And also for Medea he suffers vengeance.' [82–96]

Jason, and other characters like him in the *Inferno*, has a truly tragic
dimension. It's as if such characters are cursed by being forced to
manifest a nobility they have already essentially lost, since they are
damned—and this is the very condition of the seducer: he *manifests*
something that he cannot *be*.

One of the women seduced and abandoned by Jason was Hypsisyle, who, when the other women of the isle of Lemnos united to
massacre their menfolk, saved her father's life; another was Medea,
daughter of the king of Colchis, who has helped him obtain the
Golden Fleece. The real help and care provided by these women
challenges the illusory care the charmer Jason has been only pretending to give; his abandonment of them is thus a flight from reality as such, particularly when it takes the form of generosity.
Hypsisyle wisely rejects the female collective in its hatred of men,
but cannot see through the male one, at least not clearly enough to
avoid a charmer like Jason. And Jason must reject her because he
cannot endure any manifestation of nobility in a woman; her nur-
turing generosity torments him. The seducer may seem generous,
but his hidden parsimony is revealed by his inability to generously
receive something given in sincerity. And when Medea kills her children after Jason abandons her, it is in a desperate attempt to *become*

like him. She instinctively realizes that his seductive charm, all appearances to the contrary, hides a profound lack of care; she seems to believe that if she can become as cold and uncaring as Jason is, she can truly be his mate.

> *Thither we came, and in the moat beneath*
> *I saw a people plunged in excrement*
> *That out of human privies seemed to flow;*
> *And while there below with mine eye I searched,*
> *I saw one with his head so foul with ordure,*
> *It was not clear if he were lay or cleric.* [112–117]

These lines remind us of certain anti-clerical songs sung by the troubadours. Some are so appalled at the idea that a priest could betray his high calling that, to them, it as if he were defecating on his priesthood. 'Woe unto you, scribes and Pharisees, hypocrites! For ye are like unto whited sepulchers, which indeed appear beautiful outward, but are within full of dead men's bones, and of all uncleanness' [Matt. 23:27]. This kind of outraged piety, though entirely legitimate, is here shown as the beginning of what will later become a sacrilegious anti-clericalism.

There is no selfless flattery; flattery is always an expression of self-interest. It is, furthermore, a denial of the reality and integrity of both the flatterer and his object. That the Flatterers are covered with excrement demonstrates how the attempt to value someone or something on the basis of flattery actually degrades it.

Canto XIX

*Eighth Circle, Third Pouch, where the Simoniacs, those who bought
and sold elements of the sacred, are punished by being buried upside-
down in fiery pits.*

THE SIMONIACS represent a deeper level of fraud than the do the
flatterers, because the sin of buying and selling sacred things
directly distorts the highest spiritual reality. Such depth of fraud
requires a certain degree of insight into the truths of the Spirit. It
can sometimes happen that a person will develop in a spiritually
unbalanced way; for example, he may gain spiritual insight without
sufficient character-strength to back it up.

> *I saw upon the sides and on the bottom*
> *The livid stone with perforations filled. . . .* [13–14]

The 'livid stone' is an allusion to the 'whited sepulchers' of Matt.
23:27. The Simoniacs are buried in an inverted position because
they have inverted the spiritual hierarchy, placing material things
(their feet) in the highest place, and spiritual things (their heads) in
the lowest. The soles of their feet are scorched because they tried to
stand on the spiritual life as if it were a material substratum, thus
effectively negating it—and the negative side of the Spirit only
burns.[1] That the punishing flame passes across the soles of their feet
from heel to toe and back again shows how simony prevents the
spiritual power from moving vertically, which would help the soul
to ascend toward the Divine, but forces it to move horizontally

---

1. In our day we have seen large sums of money charged, by those following the
magical traditions of Oceania, to teach people how to walk barefoot on burning
coals. As Fr. Seraphim Rose has said, 'in our time the Devil has walked naked into
human history.'

instead. The restless, back-and-forth motion demonstrates that the spirit cannot stabilize when confined to the material level.

> *No less ample to me they seemed,* [the pits in which the
>   Simoniacs are tormented], *nor any larger*
> *Than those that in my beautiful San Giovanni*
> *Are made to serve us for baptismal fonts....* [16–18]

It is as if the pits in which the sinners are tormented were parodies of the baptismal font; the Simoniacs are horribly baptized by the fire of the Holy Spirit they sought to buy and sell.

Dante's breaking of the baptismal font [16–21] in the church of San Giovanni (St. John) 'for someone who was drowning it in' [20] represents the baptism by the Fire of the Holy Spirit which breaks the bounds of visible forms by transcending them. This shows the precedence of the Church of John the Evangelist over the Church of Peter (based on the baptism by water of John the Baptist, patron saint of Florence, for whom San Giovanni was named)—the precedence of the Spirit over the letter: 'for the letter killeth, but the spirit giveth life' [II Cor. 3:6]. It thus represents a liberation from a stifling formalism. In the words of the Baptist, from the third chapter of Matthew, verse 11, 'Indeed I baptize you with water unto repentance: but he that cometh after me ... shall baptize you with the Holy Ghost, and with fire.' As Frithjof Schuon has said:

> The Church of Peter is visible, and continuous like water; that of John—instituted on Calvary and confirmed at the Sea of Tiberias—is invisible, and discontinuous like fire. John became 'brother' of Christ and 'Son' of the Virgin, and, further, he is the prophet of the Apocalypse; Peter is charged to 'feed my sheep', but his Church seems to have inherited also his denials, whence the Renaissance and its direct and indirect consequences; however, 'the gates of hell shall not prevail against it'. John 'tarries till I come', and this mystery remains closed to Peter; one may see here a prefiguration of the 'schism' between Rome and Byzantium. 'Feed my sheep': there is nothing in these words that excludes the interpretation put upon them by the Greeks, namely, that the bishop of Rome is *primus inter pares* and not *pontifex maximus*.[2]

---

2. *Gnosis: Divine Wisdom* (Ghent: Sophia Perennis, 1990), p102.

> '*The Evangelist you Pastors had in mind,*
>   *When she who sitteth upon many waters*
>   *To fornicate with kings by him was seen;*
> *The same who with the seven heads was born,*
>   *And power and strength from the ten horns received,*
>   *So long as virtue was her husband's pleasure.*
> *Ye have made yourselves a god of gold and silver;*
>   *And from the idolater how differ ye,*
>   *Save he but one, and ye a hundred worship?*' [106–114]

The figure presented here seems to be a mixture of the Beast and the Whore of Babylon from the book of Revelations, symbolizing the Church when given over to worldly power—just as the 'Lovely Lady' [57] is the same Church when identified with Holy Wisdom [cf. 10]. The 'shepherds' who are 'husband' to the Church are the popes. Virgil shows great love for his pupil in this Canto—'he gathered me in both his arms' [124 ff]—because Dante has now begun to defend the Spirit directly, a development he has prepared himself for in [34–39]:

> *And he to me: 'If you'd have me carry you*
>   *Down there along the steepest of the banks,*
>   *From him* [a sinner they meet] *you'll know his*
>   *errors, and himself.'*
> *And I: 'Whatever pleases thee, to me is pleasing;*
>   *Thou art my Lord; thou knowest I do not swerve*
>   *From thy desire; you know what is unspoken.'*

The sinner Dante questions, who describes himself as 'a son of the she-bear' [70] is Giovanni Orsini, who became Pope Nicholas III; he waits for Pope Boniface VIII to join him in the Eighth Circle [52–53].[3]

---

3. The surname Orsini means 'she-bear'. But Nicholas III he was also a 'son of the she-bear' in a different sense. As pope, he stood as the 'pole' around which the visible Christian universe revolved, and was thus symbolically related to the polar constellations Ursa Major and Ursa Minor, the Great and Little Bears—which is why Dante describes him in line 47 as 'planted [upside down] like a pole'. Simony is an inversion of the spiritual hierarchy, and thus also of the Pole, the 'axis mundi'. As such, it is a direct violation of the 'Hyperborean' spiritual order.

Canto XX

*Eighth Circle, Fourth Pouch, reserved for the Magicians, Diviners
and Astrologers, who are not so much satanists or thaumaturges as
those who impiously sought to pierce the veil of the future. These
include Amphiarus, who foresaw his own death in the war against
Thebes, Tiresias, the soothsayer who was transformed into a woman,
and the seeress Manto.*

> *And people I saw who, through the circular valley*
> *Silent and weeping, came walking at the pace*
> *Which, in this world, holy processions take.*
> *As lower down my sight descended on them,*
> *Wondrously each one seemed to be distorted*
> *From chin to the beginning of the chest;*
> *For towards the lower back the face was turned,*
> *And backward this constrained them to advance,*
> *Even as forward sight had been denied them.* [7–15]

THESE SOULS attempted to see too far, to have greater scope (symbolized by their heads) than their degree of actualized being (represented by their bodies) would allow; they tried to *see* more than
they *were*. For them, a hellish weight replaces what, in Purgatory,
would be a kind of liturgical solemnity. These souls of Diviners and
Astrologers really do have the power to see into the future—yet their
heads are turned backwards, reminding one of a 'vanguard' cadre in
politics or an 'avant-garde' movement in the arts, which, after a few
years, turns out to be totally reactionary: their attempt to conquer
the future ultimately binds them to the past. In life they wanted to
leap out of themselves in order to see what was coming; now they

must look backwards toward what has already come to pass—and this, ultimately, is to fix their gaze on the material world alone. The material level of being is not where life comes from, but where it ends; to center one's attention there is to witness only what is receding, and consequently to immerse oneself in heaviness and melancholy.[1] To look to the future with faith in God's providence is the theological virtue of hope; to grasp after the future as these souls have done is to pervert this virtue, and therefore sink into hopelessness and despair.

In Christian terms, Jesus Christ is the call to stand in one's full humanity, and allow the Spirit of God, which includes spiritual wisdom and insight, to descend and be united with it. But the Diviners, Astrologers and Magicians, in their attempt to 'reach' the future, failed to stand where they really were ontologically. Their magical practices inflated their vision beyond their proper level of being, ultimately causing them to depart from the human form. And their denial of humanity was also a denial of Christ—the only place in their souls where the divine and the human could meet. The psyche, unless consciously subordinated to the Spirit, always becomes enslaved to matter.

> 'Here pity only lives when wholly dead;
>   For who is a greater reprobate than he
>   Who links with passion the judgment of his God?' [28–30]

These sinners pretended they could be active in relation to a passive God—who, in C.S. Lewis's words, from *Miracles: How God Intervenes in Nature and Human Affairs*, is merely 'there if you wish for Him, like a book on a shelf.' But, in reality, those aspects of the soul which were cut off from the Spirit through their practice of magic have become terribly passive; for one to believe he knows the future, or to know it actually—unless this knowledge is given by Divine Providence—is to violate and destroy one's free will.

---

1. This state of soul is perfectly expressed in Albrecht Dürer's famous engraving 'Melancholia'.

One consequence of the Magician's departure from the human form, and the resulting passivity, is that the normal sexual differentiation necessary for the continuity of life is destroyed. Tiresias manifests total gender confusion, which is a hellish distortion of life; it is this which led to the lack of male children in Greece [108–109]. The self-willed attempt to grasp the future results in a depletion of the quality of soul which would make an active engagement with life possible; the will, now forced to walk backwards, is paralyzed. Masculine activity is replaced by a quasi-feminine passivity in the face of a fated, inevitable outcome—the very opposite of the 'active receptivity' of true femininity, which, in either a man or a woman, is the soul's power to submit willingly to Divine Providence: 'Let it be done unto me according to Thy word.' [Luke 1:38]

> '. . . they all cried: "Where do you run to
> Amphiariaus? Have you quit the war?"
>   But downward still he never ceased to plunge
>   As deep as Minos, who lays hands on all.' [33–36]

Amphiaraus falls into spiritual passivity and so can no longer carry on the 'unseen warfare.' In this he resembles a degenerate liberal culture which can set no ethical standards—at least in some areas—and is thus defenseless against certain types of evil; those who believe that they have no right to be 'judgmental' have essentially given up the fight.

Amphiaraus tells the story of the founding of Mantua:

> '. . . she there, who is covering up her breasts. . . . [52]
>   Was Manto, who made quest through many lands,
> And afterwards tarried there where I was born; [55–56]
> After her father had from life departed,
>   And the city of Bacchus had become enslaved,
>   She wandered a long season through the world.
> Above in beauteous Italy lies a lake
>   At the Alp's foot that shuts in Germany
>   Over Tyrol, and has the name Benaco.
> By a thousand springs and more, I think, it's bathed,

> *Between Garda, Val Camonica and Pennino.* . . . [58–65]
> *There of necessity must fall whatever*
>   *In its bosom Benaco cannot hold,*
>   *Which flows as a river down through verdant pastures.*
> *Soon as the water doth begin to run,*
>   *No more Benaco is it called, but Mincio,*
>   *Far as Governo, where it meets the Po.*
> *Not far it runs before it finds a plain*
>   *In which it spreads itself, and makes it swampy,*
>   *Such land in summer often turns unhealthy.*
> *Traveling on that way the pitiless virgin*
>   *Discovered land surrounded by a marsh*
>   *Untilled and naked of inhabitants;*
> *There to escape all human intercourse,*
>   *She with her servants stayed, her arts to practice*
>   *And lived, and left her empty body there.*
> *The men, thereafter, who were scattered round,*
>   *Collected in that place, which was made strong*
>   *By the marsh protecting every side;*
> *They built their city over those dead bones,*
>   *And, after her who first the place selected,*
>   *Named it Mantua—no lots were cast.'* [73–93]

In this story of the origins of Virgil's home town, we can discern—
following the lead of Robert Graves in *The White Goddess*—the out-
lines of an ancient college of oracular priestesses headed by Manto;
such covens, usually nine in number, often made their homes on
river islands. The name *Manto* comes from the Greek *mantis*,
soothsayer. It is ironic [93] that no lots were cast, no divination
practiced, at the founding of a town actually named after divination; in the very place where foresight was really called for, it was
lacking. Psychic knowledge, no matter how penetrating, is always
incomplete.[2]

---

2. Line 93 also alludes to the casting of lots for Jesus' inner garment at the crucifixion, since the town of Mantua was known for the production of a fabric of the
same name, *mantua*—a word which is related, through the Latin *mantum* or *mantus*,

> *Then said he to me: 'He who from the cheek*
> > *Thrusts out his beard upon his swarthy shoulders*
> > *Was, at the time when Greece was void of males,*
> *So that hardly one remained within the cradle,*
> > *An augur in Aulis, who, along with Calchas,*
> > *Gave the propitious time to cut the cable.*
> *Eryphylus his name was, and so sings*
> > *A passage in my lofty tragedy. . . .'* [106–113]

Eurypylus is the one who divined the most auspicious time for the Greeks to sail for Troy; he was certainly right, in a sense, since the Greeks were victorious. But from Virgil's point of view, as expressed in the *Aeneid*, the Trojans—those who lost the war, but went on to found Rome—would represent the hidden spiritual center in that situation; though the psychic Eurypylus could see future events, he could not see their true spiritual import.

> *Behold the wretched ones, who left their needle,*
> > *Their spool and spindle, and took up fortune-telling;*
> *They cast their magic spells with herb and image.*
> > > > > [121–123]

The women who leave needle, spool and spindle, like Helen did, have left the basis of their lives—a basis that Penelope remained faithful to. This feminine life-center may seem unimaginative to some, but it is nonetheless truly constructive and close to the subtle pattern of things. To depart from it, as so many women are now being forced to do, is often to follow flights of fantasy which ultimately unravel not only the form of a woman's life, but her soul as well.

---

to our word *mantle*. Fate or the pattern of life is often traditionally compared to a woven fabric, like those made by Helen and Penelope in the *Iliad* and *Odyssey*. As opposed to the saving grace available to Christians through the atonement, which has the power to change the pattern of life, fate for the pagan is always a closed system; his fate is always sealed.

'And yesternight the moon was round already;
   Thou shouldst remember well it did not harm thee
   Those times you saw it within the forest deep.' [127–129]

Psychic knowledge is, nonetheless, a reflection of Spiritual knowledge, as the moon reflects the light of the Sun; it is certainly not all
evil or delusive, but it requires Spiritual knowledge to center it.

Canto XXI

Eighth Circle, Fifth Pouch, where the Barrators—buyers and sellers of public office—and the Embezzlers are punished by being immersed in boiling pitch; Dante compares them to tar-stained shipwrights. The travelers fall in with a gang of punishing demons, the Male-branche.

THE SPACE OF THE BARRATORS (traffickers in public office) and the Embezzlers is visibly dark and obscure. The demon the travelers meet gives them false directions, like those used by secret criminals to cover up their crimes. The 'stew' [8] where the sinners are boiled in black pitch is an apt symbol of embezzlement and graft, where everything must be done in darkness, 'under the table'. By nature these sins are sticky and opaque.

Dante compares the boiling pitch to that used to caulk ships in dry-dock at the arsenal in Venice. The Venetian shipwrights he describes were perhaps organically connected, in a mysterious way, to this level of Hell, not necessarily in their souls but rather by virtue of their outward appearance. As God says in the Koran, 'We shall show them Our signs in the horizons [i.e., the outer world] and in themselves' [41:53]; the objects of the visible world, by their beauty or their ugliness, are all symbols of inner realities. In the words of Maximos the Confessor:

> The world is one . . . for the spiritual world in its totality is man-
> ifested in the totality of the perceptible world, mystically
> expressed in symbolic pictures for those who have eyes to see.
> And the perceptible world in its entirety is secretly fathomable by
> the spiritual world in its entirety, when it has been simplified and
> amalgamated by means of the spiritual realities. The former is

embodied in the latter through the realities; the latter in the former through the symbols. The operation of the two is one.[1]

These tar-stained workmen repairing worn-out ships are 'making their way' through life by scorn and vulgarity, which are inseparable from the type of sin the shipwrights symbolize; their contempt for others renders them disgusting.[2]

When Dante says,

> *Then I turned, like one who is impatient*
>   *To know the thing he flees from, and is struck*
>   *By sudden shock and terror at what he sees*
> *And who, while looking, does not delay his flight.* . . . [25–28]

it indicates that he is on the edge of a dangerous fascination with an evil he must avoid; secrecy attracts curiosity. (When he expresses a similar fascination in lines 127–135, Virgil advises him to ignore what he sees.)

> *Then I beheld behind us a pitch-black devil,*
>   *Running along upon the crag, approach*
> *Ah, how ferocious was he in his aspect!*
>   *And how he seemed to me in action ruthless,*
>   *With open wings, with lithe and agile feet!*
> *Across each shoulder, sharp-pointed and high,*
>   *A sinner he carried, doubled at the hip*
> *And gripped him by the sinews of his feet.* [29–36]

Here evil is beginning to gain the ascendancy. It no longer shows only weakness, but has begun to manifest an inverted power— hence the demon's swiftness. Grafters must act fast to make the most of their opportunities, but since they are forced to operate

---

1. *Mystogogia*, 2 (PG 91, 669), quoted in Clément, *The Roots of Christian Mysticism*, p 219.

2. Dante's name for this type of sinner is *barratier*. The word 'barrator' in English denotes either one who buys and sells public office, or a sea captain or crew member who defrauds the owner of a ship or of its cargo.

'underground,' this speed hides a terrible burden beneath it. The demons now have the names of dogs: *Cagnazzo* ('big dog') and *Graffiacane* ('dog-scratcher'). And the black demon is compared [44–45] to a mastiff unleashed to catch a thief; we are in the realm of 'dog eat dog' [cf. 131].[3]

> *They issued from beneath the little bridge,*
> *   And turned against him all their grappling-irons;*
> *   But he cried out: 'Let all restrain their anger!*
> *Before those hooks of yours lay hold of me,*
> *   Let one of you step forward, now, and listen,*
> *   And then decide if I am to be hooked.'*
> *They all cried out: 'Let Malacoda go';*
> *   Whereat one started, and the rest stood still,*
> *   He came up to him, saying: 'What use is this?'*
> *'Do you really think, Malacoda, you'd have seen me*
> *   Walk straight into this place,' my Master said,*
> *   'Forearmed so well against all your obstacles,*
> *Without the help of God and auspicious fate?*
> *   Let me go on, for in Heaven it is willed*
> *   That to another I point out the savage road.'*
> *And then the pride of Malacoda fell. . . .* [70–85]

> *And unto me my Guide: 'O thou, who sittest*
> *   Crouched down among the splinters of the bridge,*
> *   Safely you may now return to me.'*
> *Wherefore I started and came swiftly to him. . . .* [88–91]

Here the demons are shown as having the power to hide the good, or to make it hide, but not the power to destroy it.

> *And all the devils forward thrust themselves,*
> *So that I feared they would not keep their promise.*

---

3. These were actual family names in the region of Lucca; they sound surprisingly like the kind of criminal nicknames later used by the *Mafiosi*. The surname *Lucchese*, meaning 'from Lucca,' is that of a present-day Mafia family.

Thus afraid I once beheld the soldiers
Who came out under safeguard from Caprona,
Seeing themselves among so many foes. [92–96]

Dante recalls the image of the infantry leaving Caprona, as well as that of the arsenal at Venice, because he is now beginning to encounter the *reign* of evil, which has something militaristic about it. Under a regime of graft the simple, honest man with a petition is at a disadvantage; if he is wise, he will hide his need. That Dante and Virgil must confer secretly [2–3], and that Virgil cautions him, 'Don't let/Those demons see you; here, crouch down/Behind this crag, and give yourself some cover. ...' [58–60] reveals this to be the place where the good must go under cover, because here evil is organized. But though it has now become conspiratorial, it has no real center; as it says in line 48 'The Sacred Face [symbol of the Center] has no place here.'

Here is where the devils show *fear* for the first time—fear of the good. The lower the level of Hell the travelers reach, the closer they are to Hell's end. The Inferno is now so dark that the good can appear *as* good: 'The light shineth in the darkness and the darkness comprehended it not.' [John 1:5]

'Pursue your way along this rocky edge;
Near is another crag that forms a path.' [110–111]

This is the first direct lie told in the *Inferno*, a lie of misdirection. The demons tell Virgil and Dante to climb *up* and connect with a different ridge if they want to proceed—but in CANTO XXIII, line 49, Virgil must quickly snatch Dante and slide *down* to escape them, and pass on to the next pouch. The demons exhibit *hubris* here, as if it were within their power, and also within their rights, to create an alternate reality, to 'change a *no* to a *yes*' in the words of line 42. But beneath this *hubris* is the same fear of the good, which is also a fear of the truth.

'Yesterday, five hours later than this hour,
One thousand and two hundred sixty-six
Years were finished since this road was broken.' [112–114]

The demon wants to make it appear as if Christ's harrowing of Hell has blocked the path for Virgil and Dante—but what it has actually done is prevent the sinners in the higher circles from sinking even lower, this being a distant reflection of the Atonement.

In this pouch the anal aspect of homosexual dominance-and-submission makes its appearance, symbolized by the demon Malacoda, 'bad-tail'. 'Shall I jab him . . . in the rump? 'Yes' . . . you'd better let him have it!' [101–102]; 'And he [Barbariccia, 'curly-bearded', perhaps an allusion to pubic hair] had made a trumpet of his rump' [139]. Here is the pouch where sinners practice 'brown-nosing' to gain advantage, where they 'screw each other' for power.

> 'I've sent ten of my company in that direction
> To see if any sinner sniffs for air.' [115–116]

Here Malacoda dispatches ten of his demons to police the tormented sinners; these ten are the Ten Commandments in inverted form. Organized evil is here shown as a kind of perversion of sacred Law.

> 'Ah me! what is it, Master, that I see?
>   Pray let us go,' I said, 'without an escort,
>   If thou knowest how, since I ask none for myself.
> If thou art vigilant, as is thy habit,
>   Dost thou not witness how they gnash their teeth,
>   And with their brows are threatening us with harm?'
> And he to me: 'I will not have thee fear;
>   Let them gnash on, according to their fancy;
>   They do it for those wretches boiling in the pitch.' [126–135]

There is a 'sticky' power of fascination in evil which draws one toward it by identification as a vacuum draws air, as a privation of reality depletes one's spirit. Dante's fear indicates that he has a tendency to identify with this particular sin, which is why Virgil advises him not to pay it any mind; he must learn to ignore it.[4]

---

4. Dante was actually accused of the crime of barratry by his political opponents, the Black Guelphs.

Canto XXII

Still the Eighth Circle, Fifth Pouch. More Barrators. Ciampolo tricks the demons.

THE DEMONS' SIGNAL TO BEGIN their march to escort Dante and Virgil through the Eighth Circle is a fart given by Barbariccia in the last line of the preceding CANTO:

> *We went upon our way with those ten demons;*
> *Savage company! And yet 'in the church*
> *With the saints, in the tavern with the gluttons'!* [13–15]

As in the preceding canto, the *Inferno* here exhibits a kind of comic element. The manifestations of evil are becoming more horrible as we descend, but we are also drawing closer to the point where evil can be overcome—as witness the ability of the Navarese sinner to deceive the demons. The damned soul cannot redeem himself, of course, but this ability to trick his prison guards is like an infernal reflection of hope—a precursor to the point in CANTO XXVI where Ulysses begins to speak of Purgatory. (Ulysses is not walking the path of salvation, but at least he knows it exists.) Those in higher circles, though in less infernal states, are too enfolded in Hell to even let themselves be conscious of the possibility of Purgation. Here we see how evil, as it worsens, uses itself up in a sense; it no longer appears quite so absolute.

In both Purgatory and Paradise, higher states of being are higher in every sense: they are closer to Reality. In ascending through them, one draws nearer to their principle, which is the Sovereign Good. But in Hell, the closer one gets to its most hideous, most hellish parts, the areas where existence is the most unbearable, the nearer one has come to letting the good break through. The irony is that Satan, situated at the pit of hell, the center of evil, cannot prevent Dante and Virgil from setting foot on the steps of Purgatory, or even delay them (as in Hell's higher circles), because Satan is paralyzed. His body even becomes their road. As compared to Purgatory and Paradise, Hell, since it represents a privation of reality, is *not itself.*

> 'Ah me! see that one, how he grinds his teeth;
>   I would have more to say, but am afraid
>   He might be getting ready to scratch my itch.'
> Then the grand Provost, facing Farfarello,
>   Who rolled his eyes about as if to strike,
>   Said: 'Stand aside there, thou malicious bird.'
> 'If you desire either to see or hear,'
>   After this the frightened one resumed,
>   'Tuscans or Lombards, I will make them come.
> But let the Malebranche stand aside,
>   So that these may not their vengeance fear,
>   And I, down sitting in this very place,
> Though I be one I will make seven come,
>   When I shall whistle, as our custom is
>   When one of us had managed to get out.'
> Cagnazzo at these words his muzzle lifted,
>   Shaking his head, and said: 'Just hear the trick
>   Which he thinks might let him dive back in!'
> To this he who was rich in artifice,
>   Responded: 'Then I must have too many tricks
>   If by them I bring more suffering to my people.'
> Then Alichino could not contain himself,
>   But, counter to the others, said to him:
>   'I will not gallop after you if you dive
> But beat my wings instead above the pitch;
>   We'll leave the height, and with the bank to shield us
>   We'll see if you can handle all of us alone!'
> And now, my reader, listen to this new sport:
>   Each turned his eyes toward the other shore
>   He first, who'd been most hesitant before;

The Navarrese selected well his time;
 Planted his feet on land, and in a moment
 Leaped, and released himself from their design.
Upon this, all the demons became crestfallen,
 But he the most who was cause of their defeat;
 He lept and cried 'I've got you' to hide his shame;
Little good it did him, his wings could not
 Outfly his victim's fear, who soon went under;
 The other, rising up again, lifted his chest;
Not otherwise will a wild duck quickly dive
 When he sees the falcon drawing near, and then
 Fly up again, exasperated and weary.
Enraged at the one who mocked him, Calcabrina
 Flew close behind him, glad to let the sinner
 Escape from him, if by that he could pick a fight.
So when the barrator had disappeared,
 He turned his talons on his friend instead,
 And grappled with him right above the moat.
But Alichino was indeed a mighty hawk;
 He clawed him well, until the both of them
 Fell in the middle of the boiling pond. [91–141]

Barratry is graft, and graft involves a pretense of offering help—which is, of course, a lie. It is a perversion of the virtues of charity and loyalty [99–111]. This condition is a precursor to the Ninth Circle of Hell, the last one, which is based on the perversion of friendship and true love. Here the Navarrese turns the demons' anger away from himself and toward each other, which is exactly what happens when a destructive psychological complex ends by destroying itself. This self-decon-struction of a complex takes place on the psychic level alone, however, and such psychic purgation can only happen in a real and fruitful way under the influence of the Spirit, which is absent here. The Navarrese's trick is a shadow and parody of *detachment*—but it is without spiritual effect, since the Navarrese is damned. Here we see how, as deeper levels of Hell are reached, the damned have more *character*—understandably, since the more grievous sins are the more deliberate ones, which are worse than simple passions or weaknesses.

Canto XXIII

Still in the Fifth Pouch of the Eighth Circle. Pursued by demons, Virgil seizes Dante and slides with him down into the Sixth Pouch. Here the Hypocrites are punished by being forced to wear leaden capes plated with gold.

> *Silent, alone, and without company*
> *We went, the one in front, the other after,*
> *As go the Minor Friars along their way.* [1–3]

THE SILENCE AND ALONENESS represent Unity; that 'one went before, one after' symbolizes precedence, hierarchy—Unity and hierarchy being the two prime aspects of the spiritual order. The first is realized through detachment, the second through humility.

> '... *Master, if thou hidest not*
> *Thyself and me forthwith, of Malebranche*
> *I am in dread; we have them now behind us;*
> *I imagine them so clearly, I sense them already.'* [22–24]

In this Canto, the travelers encounter fear. On the one hand, Dante's fear of the demons is simply 'in his mind'—as when, in line 33, Virgil speaks of 'escape from this imagined chase.' On the other hand, it is also very real. Negatively, this is paranoia; we often call up in imagination the events we fear to encounter. (This is the final outcome of fantasy, which is a wandering of the imagination into areas of diminished reality: the evil is always less real than the Good.) Positively, however, this power of imagination allows Dante to conceive of Virgil's reality as spiritual Guide on a deeper level than before. What we call *projection* is much more than modern psychology will admit to. It is not simply an illusion in the negative sense; we must subjectively imagine what is objectively true in order to realize it. The mystery here is that Virgil is a true Guide, even though the Virgil that Dante follows through Hell is, in another way, merely an image in his own mind. Dante's image of Virgil partakes of the archetype of the spiritual Guide far more profoundly than his image of another man would, even if that man were present in the flesh. As Dante looks toward Virgil through the power of spiritual, objective imagination, his true identity is more and more clearly revealed.[1] The more deeply he sees Virgil, the more deeply he is seen.

> '. . . *If I were a leaded mirror,*
> *I would not have power to attract your outer image*
> *More swiftly than I have just received your inner.*
> *Even now your thoughts come in among my own;*

1. As William Chittick points out in *Imaginal Worlds: Ibn al-'Arabi and the Problem of Religious Diversity* (Cambridge: Islamic Texts Society, 1990), 'human knowledge of God is determined by the human capacity to know Him. "God discloses Himself to the created thing only in the form of the created thing"' (Ibn al-'Arabi, *al-Futuhat al-Makkiyya* IV 110.7) That divine self-disclosure is the person's Lord, because it determines his destiny in this world and in every world to come, for all eternity.' [p151] The same perspective appears in Ps. 110:6: 'The Lord [the Godhead] said unto my Lord [the particular 'Lord' of David, his 'God created in belief'], Sit thou at my right hand, until I make thy enemies thy footstool.' In the words of Henry Corbin, from *Creative Imagination in the Sufism of Ibn 'Arabi*:

> the Creation is essentially a *theophany* (*tajalli*). As such, Creation is an act of the divine imaginative power: the divine creative Imagination is essentially a theophanic Imagination. The Active Imagination in the gnostic is likewise a theophanic Imagination; the beings it 'creates' subsist with an independent existence *sui generis* in the intermediate world which pertains to this mode of existence. The God whom it 'creates,' far from being an unreal product of our fantasy, is also a Theophany, for man's Active Imagination is merely the organ of the absolute theophanic Imagination (*takhayyul mutlaq*). Prayer is a theophany par excellence; as such, it is 'creative'; but the God to whom it is addressed because it 'creates' Him is precisely the God who reveals Himself to Prayer in this Creation, and this Creation, at this moment, is one among the theophanies whose real Subject is the Godhead revealing Himself to Himself. [pp182–183]

Virgil, as well as the Beatrice and St. Bernard of the *Paradiso*, are thus imagined figures of a real Divine Guidance created in the soul of Dante by the Divine Poetic Imagination operating within him.

> *They appear the same in action, the same in face*
> *So that out of both I've come to one decision.*
> *If by chance the right bank is not too steep*
> *We can used it to climb down to the next moat;*
> *Thus shall we escape from this imagined chase.'* [25–33]

Here we see how identity extends beyond the ego when the ego dies.

The leaded mirror receives Dante's outer image because, in alchemical terminology, lead represents unredeemed matter, as opposed to gold which is matter transmuted by the Spirit. The implication here is that Virgil, as the inverse of the Hypocrites, is lead without and golden within. And Virgil has also received Dante's inner image; his spiritual Heart mirrors Dante's essence, this being the function of the spiritual Guide.

When Virgil says, 'So that out of both [our thoughts] I've come to one decision,' he is alluding to different levels of reality and the relationship between them—in this case, the personal and the archetypal. Here is where Virgil, the archetypal poet of Rome, fully appears as Dante's prototype, and Dante as his true protégé. Dante became the national poet of Italy as well as the 'imperial' poet of Roman Christendom; thus he is as legitimately a student and spiritual son of Virgil as anyone living in Virgil's time could possibly have been [cf. 51]. Here is expressed the mystery of the relationship—both in terms of identity and of polarity—between the visible and the invisible; in this world of visible realities 'we see in part, as in a dark mirror,' while in the archetypal world we see 'face to face'. In one way Virgil represents the invisible and Dante the visible dimension, because Dante appears as the living author and protagonist of the *Commedia*, and Virgil as the poet's mental image. But on another level Virgil fully manifests the archetype of national poet, and so relates to the visible, while Dante, as he writes these lines, is only national poet *in potentia*; his future fame is still invisible to outer eyes.

The spiritual Guide has the responsibility of accepting his pupils' projections. In a simple way you could say that Dante is psychologically projecting on Virgil, and the one projecting always projects an aspect of himself. But in a deeper way, this projection shows Dante and Virgil as participating in a common Reality. What Dante sees of Virgil really *is* the true Virgil—but it is also a projection of the true Dante, since Virgil is Dante's Self. The invisible allows the visible to appear as itself: 'Not that any one has seen the Father' [John 6:46], and yet 'he that hath seen Me hath seen the Father.' [John 14:9] This is the essence of spiritual guidance.

> *Never ran so swiftly water through a sluice*
>   *To turn the wheel of any land-built mill. . . .*
> *As did my Master down along that border,*
>   *Bearing me with him upon his breast,*
>   *As his own son, and not as a companion.* [46–51]

The mill, which refines grain and prepares it for transformation into edible food, is related to the sublimation and refinement of dark feelings. Here Virgil is carrying Dante out of spiritual danger, and this motion also 'turns the mill' that enables him to do the spiritual and emotional work necessary to compose the *Commedia*.

> *A painted people down below we found,*
>   *Who circled there with footsteps very slow,*
>   *Weeping and in their semblance tired and vanquished.*
> *They had on mantles with the hoods low down*
>   *Before their eyes, and fashioned of the cut*
>   *That's used to make the robes for Cluny's monks.*
> *On the outside they're so gilded that it dazzles;*
>   *But inwardly all leaden, and so heavy*
>   *That Frederick's capes were straw compared with them.*
> *Exhausting mantle for eternity!* [58–67]

✠

Dante and Virgil now encounter the Hypocrites.

The Hypocrites are those who, unlike the true spiritual Guide, depend upon the projections of others in order to maintain their aura of sanctity. They have indulged in 'spiritual *chic*'—the robes of the monks at Cluny were known for their stylishness—and are now being punished for it.[2]

That their cloaks are gold without and lead within demonstrates that even though they have a certain ability to manifest the Spirit, the whole import of the Spirit is for them materialistic; they only value the Spirit in material terms.

The Hypocrites are punished by the burden of *heaviness*. In Paradise the souls are supple and have the ability to fly. But the Hypocrites have put so much spiritual energy into surface appearances which *seem* supple in this world—into glamour, in other words—that now, in the afterlife, they are weighted down by the very glittering surface that once seemed so light. Lead is heavier in Hell because the sinking or *tamasic* quality of matter is more powerful there— whereas in Paradise, matter is transubstantiated.

> '. . . *These yellow cloaks*
> *Are made of lead so heavy, that their weight*
> *Makes us, the balances underneath them, creak.*' [100–102]

But balance is the very thing the soul of the hypocrite lacks. The balance of inner and outer is so radically disturbed that the inner man is ultimately sacrificed for the outer.

The balance is not redressed, however, by giving equal weight to

---

2. The same opposition of lead and gold in terms of hypocrisy and sincerity appears in Shakespeare's *The Merchant of Venice*, where Portia's image—love's true gold, the objective or *theophanic* aspect of the imagination [cf. Henry Corbin, *Creative Imagination in the Sufism of Ibn 'Arabi*]—is hidden within a leaden casket, while the golden casket, chosen by her shallowest, most flamboyant suitor, only conceals the following verses:

> All that glisters is not gold;—
> Often have you heard that told:
> Many a man his life hath sold
> But my outside to behold:
> Gilded tombs do worms infold.
> Had you been as wise as bold,
> Young in limbs, in judgement old,
> Your answer had not been inscroll'd:
> Fare you well; your suit is cold.

both sides; one re-establishes balance between inner and outer by becoming more inner, since the inner reality always has precedence. According to Frithjof Schuon,

> To the question: 'What is sin?' it may be replied that this term refers to two levels or dimensions: the first of these requires that one should 'obey the commandments,' and the second, in accordance with the words of Christ to the rich young man, that one should 'follow Me,' which is to say, that one should establish oneself in the 'inward dimension' and so realize contemplative perfection; the example of Mary takes precedence over that of Martha. Now, suffering in the world is due not only to sin in the elementary sense of the word, but above all to the sin of 'outwardness,' which moreover fatally gives rise to all the others.[3]

The outer should pick up the reflection of the inner, not usurp its place. By calling themselves 'balances', which is the last thing they really are, these sinners clearly show that they are still Hypocrites.

What is false often seems more plausible than what is true, on the level of appearances, and therefore tends to confer certain advantages in this world, at least to begin with. The con artist will commonly look more sincere than the honest man—as was demonstrated above in the figure of Geryon, whose flight is the symbol of a hypocritical suppleness. The hypocrite can put all his psychic energy into appearing sincere because he is not constrained by the truth, while an honest man in the same circumstances will often manifest an entirely appropriate reticence—which the hypocrite will then attempt to portray as shiftiness or dishonesty. Frithjof Schuon has this to say about a hypocritical sincerity—'sincerism'—which runs counter to objective truth:

> Sincerism ... flies to defend all things blameworthy, whether extravagant and pernicious or simply mediocre and vulgar; in short, to be 'sincere' is to show oneself 'as one is,' unconditionally and cynically, hence counter to any effort to be what one ought

---

3. *The Transfiguration of Man* (Bloomington, IN: World Wisdom Books, 1995), p39.

to be. It is forgotten that the worth of sincerity lies in its contents only, and that it is charity to avoid giving a bad example; the individual owes society a correct comportment, to say the least, which has nothing to do with the vice of dissimulation. Let us specify that correct comportment, such as is required by good sense and traditional morality, has as a necessary corollary a certain effacement, whereas hypocrisy by definition is a kind of exhibitionism, crude or subtle as the case may be.[4]

Both cynicism and hypocrisy are forms of pride; cynicism is the caricature of sincerity or frankness, while hypocrisy is the caricature of scrupulousness or self-discipline or of virtue in general. Cynics believe that sincerity consists in exhibiting shortcomings and that to hide them is to be a hypocrite; they do not master themselves and still less do they seek to transcend themselves; and the fact that they take their fault for a virtue is clear proof of their pride. Hypocrites believe, on the other hand, that it is virtuous to make a display of virtuous attitudes or that the appearances of faith suffice for faith itself; their vice lies, not in manifesting the forms of virtue – which is a rule that must apply to everyone – but in believing that the manifestation is virtue itself and, above all, in aping virtue in the hope of being admired: this is pride, because it is individualism and ostentation. Pride is to overestimate oneself and to underestimate others; and this is what the cynic does just as much as the hypocrite, in a blatant or subtle way as the case may be.

All this amounts to saying that in cynicism as in hypocrisy, the self-willed and therefore tenebrous ego takes the place of the spirit and of light; these two vices are acts of theft by which the passional and egotistic soul appropriates what belongs to the spiritual soul. Moreover, to present a vice as a virtue and, correspondingly, to accuse virtues of being vices, as is done by cynicism posing as sincerity, is nothing but hypocrisy; and it is a particularly perverse hypocrisy.[5]

---

4. *The Play of Masks* (Bloomington, IN: World Wisdom Books, 1992), p 64.
5. *Esoterism as Principle and as Way* (Ghent, NY: Sophia Perennis, 1992), pp 123–4.

Dante is accosted by two of the hypocrites; he asks them who they are:

> *'Jovial Friars were we, and Bolognese;*
> *I Catalano, and he Loderingo*
> *These were our names; both chosen by your city,*
> *For a post that's usually held by only one,*
> *For the keeping of its peace; and what we were*
> *Is still there to be seen around Gardingo.'* [103–108]

Hypocrisy is a false reconciliation between incompatible values, as if balance could be re-established by treating inner and outer, or Spirit and matter, as equals. To do so is always to give the edge to matter, however, because a person's ignorance of the hierarchical relation between Spirit and matter indicates that his criteria for evaluation are already quantitative, and thus materialistic. Spirit and matter can be rebalanced only by giving precedence to the Spirit. This wrong-headed attempt to place the greater and lesser on the same level is represented by the souls of Catalano and Loderingo, a Guelph and a Ghibelline, who were given joint authority in Florence in order to establish peace between the two parties—a move which only led to greater violence.

> *'... This impaled one, whom thou seest,*
> *Advised the Pharisees that it was best*
> *To let one suffer instead of a whole people*
> *Crosswise and naked is he on the path,*
> *As thou perceivest; and lying helpless there*
> *He must weigh the mass of whoever walks upon him.'*
> [115–120]

Caiaphas is crucified horizontally. This means that he is forced to suffer the contradictions within his soul (this being the essence of crucifixion, the state of being 'crossed') without access to the vertical dimension which alone could reconcile them; his suffering does not open him to Grace. According to the Christian idea, suffering is precisely what ultimately opens one to the grace of God. The suffering of Caiaphas doesn't have this power, however, because in judging and condemning Jesus he denied the very Person who could perfectly suffer in this way—and by denying the unique personhood of Christ, who is also the Christ within each of us, he also denied the dimension of unique personhood *per se* in the name of a collectivity. The drama of the condemnation and crucifixion of Christ is the precise archetype of this denial.

The crucifixion of Caiaphas represents an inversion of the conscious bearing of burdens that is the essence of vertical or spiritual crucifixion. The Christian takes suffering upon himself willingly, even if it is a suffering that he or she cannot avoid. It is this conscious decision that opens Christian suffering to Heaven, and allows its burdens gradually to be lightened. But Caiaphas, in denying Christ, has repudiated the very part of himself that could suffer in this way.

> *And thereupon I saw my Virgil marvel*
> *At him who was extended on the cross*
> *So vilely, in eternal banishment.* [124–126]

Virgil, a pagan, clearly sees the lack of Christian truth in Caiaphas— and so (by inversion, which is all that is allowed in Hell) he implicitly sees Christian truth in its positive depth.

> *The Leader stood awhile with head bowed down;*
> *Then said: 'He gave a false account of the business*
> *Who grapples with his hook the sinners yonder.'*
> *And the Friar: 'Many of the Devil's vices*
> *I once heard about at Bologna, and among them,*
> *That he's a liar and the father of it.'*
> *Thereat my Leader with great strides went on,*
> *Somewhat disturbed, with anger in his looks....* [139–146]

Virgil demonstrates here that he also understands the consequences of false spiritual guidance; as the Sufis say, 'he who has no Guide has Satan for a guide.' As a pagan acting as Guide for a Christian, he is beginning to feel his lack of relationship to Christ.

Canto XXIV

*From the Eighth Circle, Sixth Pouch, the inferno of the Hypocrites, to
the Eighth Circle, Seventh Pouch, the inferno of the Thieves, who are
tormented by serpents.*

In that part of the youthful year wherein
  The Sun beneath Aquarius warms his locks,
  And when the nights draw near to half a day;
What time the hoar-frost copies on the ground
  The outward semblance of her sister white,
  But not for long, so dull the pen he wields.
The farmer who is short of forage rises,
  And looks, and stares, and seeing all his fields
  In gleaming white, he beats upon his thigh,
Goes back indoors, and up and down laments,
  Like a poor wretch, who knows not what to do;
  But when he looks again, his hopes revive
Seeing the world has changed its countenance
  So quickly; so he takes his shepherd's crook,
  And forth the little lambs to pasture drives.
Thus did the Master fill me with alarm,
  When I beheld his forehead so disturbed,
  Yet to the ailment came as soon the cure. [1–18]

HERE THE DESPAIR of having to face evil directly makes its appearance, and must be overcome through spiritual effort. Dante and Virgil were almost frozen by their encounter with hypocrisy—which requires one to turn a cold eye toward glamorous seduction in order to see through it—but they broke away: what seemed to be deep snow was only a morning's frost.

> *And even as he who ponders as he labors,*
> *And is always well prepared for the next step*
> *While upward lifting me towards the summit*
> *Of an enormous rock, he surveyed another crag,*
> *And said to me: 'Take hold of that one next,*
> *But try it first to see if it will hold.'*
> *This was no path for someone in a cloak;*
> *For barely could we—he light, and I supported—*
> *Manage to climb the slope from spur to spur.* [25–33]

Climbing here is another foretaste of Purgatory, since effort is required, and effort is rewarded in Purgatory, though never in Hell.

Despite all its glamorous pretensions, hypocrisy is heavy. Since it is a form of illusion, we think the way to defeat it is by becoming more grounded. But the travelers have to *climb out* of the pouch of the Hypocrites; they must elevate themselves above it spiritually. Dante is still mortal, still struggling with the passions of terrestrial existence; in order to escape hypocrisy he must be supported by Virgil, who possesses the lightness of immortality, the nearest approach to spiritual reality possible in Hell.

Guided by Virgil, Dante must pick his steps with care. Hypocrisy diverts a person's attention from what he should be doing in the present moment; it causes him to fall back on what he already has. Hypocrites 'pontificate' but they do not perceive; hypocrisy requires both effort and perception to overcome it.

> *'It is now required of you to put off sloth,'*
> *My Master said; 'for he who rests on down,*
> *Or under quilt, can never come to fame. . . .'* [46–48]

Fame here symbolizes, or suggests, immortality, though the only image of immortality possible in Hell is that of 'poetic immortality,' which is mortal memory. Hypocrisy relies upon what is already established, either by others or by oneself at an earlier stage of one's life, as when a poet or other professional will be tempted to 'rest on his laurels.' It is related to complacency, and is therefore opposed to spiritual effort. Hypocrisy is a form of pride, which St. Augustine characterizes in the following way: 'All the other sins attach themselves to vices; only pride attaches itself to the virtues, in order to destroy them.'

> 'Whoever without renown his life consumes
> Such vestige leaveth of himself on earth,
> As smoke in air, or in the water, foam.' [49–51]

A person such as the one Virgil describes is invested in ephemerality; he has 'built his house on sand'. He is so engrossed in phenomena that he believes the passing scene to be the only reality, and so has lost touch with his own true nature.

> 'Stand up, therefore, and overcome your anguish
> With such spirit as triumphs in every battle,
> Unless it sinks beneath its body's weight.' [52–54]

Hypocrites cling to form, but the Spirit is always a little beyond form; the body, again, is what is already established.

> 'A longer stairway yet you still must mount;
> 'Tis not enough from these to have departed;
> If you understand me, may it do you good.'
> Then I uprose and showed myself provided
> Better with breath than I had been before. . . . [55–59]

Simply criticizing hypocrisy is not enough to prevent one from being a hypocrite. A person must also commit to living on the plane of the Spirit, here symbolized by *breath*. Spiritual reality, objective reality, is the breath of life.

> . . . a voice from the next moat came forth,
> Not well adapted to articulate words. [65–66]

The damned souls, in losing the power of speech, are actually beginning to depart from the human form (as opposed to the Gluttons, for example, who have only distorted it). They are becoming animalistic, subhuman.

> *I was bent downward, but my living eyes*
> > *Could not make out the bottom through the dark;*
> > *Wherefore I: 'Master, I hope we can arrive*
> *At the next circle, then move on down the wall;*
> > *For as I hear but cannot understand,*
> > *So I look down but can distinguish nothing.'*
> *He said, 'No other answer will I give you*
> > *But action itself, for a fair request*
> > *Ought to be followed in silence by the deed.'* [70–78]

Inarticulate souls and impenetrable darkness betoken chaos. *Order* here is in Dante's act alone, not in his foresight. The effort Dante has already made [22–30] has trained and prepared his will, so that here he can act swiftly in response to guidance without first needing to understand it.

> *. . . I beheld therein a terrible throng*
> > *Of serpents, and of such a monstrous kind,*
> > *That memory of them still congeals my blood.*
> *Let Libya boast no longer of her sands. . . .* [82–85]
> *Neither so many plagues nor so malignant*
> > *Ever showed she, with all of Ethiopia,*
> > *And all the lands that border the Red Sea!*
> *Among this cruel and most dismal throng*
> > *People were running naked and in terror,*
> > *Without the hope of hole or heliotrope.*
> *They had their hands with serpents bound behind them;*
> > *These thrust both head and tail right through their loins*
> > *And were tied together on the other side.*
> *And lo! at one who was upon our side*
> > *There darted forth a serpent, which transfixed him*
> > *There where the neck is knotted to the shoulders.*
> *Never was so quickly written an 'O' or 'I',*
> > *As he took fire, and burned; and as he fell*
> > *The sinner was completely changed to ashes.*
> *And when he on the ground lay thus destroyed,*
> > *The ashes drew together, and of themselves*

Back to his former self they quickly turned.
According to the great sages, in just this way
  The phoenix dies, and then is born again,
  When it approaches its five-hundredth year. . . . [88–108]

And just as he who falls, and knows not how,
  By force of demons who drag him to the earth
  Or by some other hindrance binding man,
When he arises and around him looks,
  Wholly bewildered by the mighty anguish
  Which he has suffered, and in looking sighs;
Such seemed that sinner after he had risen. [112–118]

That the snakes are from the lands bordering Egypt represents a
kind of perversion of spiritual energy, as may actually have happened in the Egyptian religion when spiritual realization descended
into magic. The primal theft was Eve's theft of the forbidden fruit.
Tempted by the serpent, she took something from the Divine realm
and enclosed it within the human one; she did not wait for that
divine knowledge to be revealed to her in its own terms and in its
own time. This theft of knowledge caused such a disequilibrium in
the cosmos that Adam and Eve lost the Terrestrial Paradise. Through
merely human means they destroyed their relationship to Paradise,
but they could not re-establish it through human means, since
angels now guard the gates. Man can descend but not ascend on his
own power, because his very existence is a gift of God; he can squan-
der, but he cannot earn. In Christian terms, only the redemption of
fallen existence by Jesus Christ, the grace of which is conferred by
the sacrament of baptism, can return man to his original state.

Theft, more than any other sin, is involved with concealment, since
both the act and the stolen goods must be hidden—which is why the
sinners here are naked, *exposed*. We are now entering more deeply into
realms of illusion and deceit: the true identity of the thieves is revealed
here, along with their inconstancy. For the snakes to be so centered in
the lower part of the sinners' bodies represents a destruction of
spiritual potential: since the spiritual realm has been entirely cut off, it
is as if the spirit, or a parody thereof, turns into a snake, because it can

only now exist on that lower level which the figure of the snake symbolizes; but since it is fundamentally at odds with that lower level, it can only attack it. That the snake strikes the sinner where his neck joins his shoulders represents the severing of the imagination (the head) from reality (the body). A bodiless head can no longer rule the body, and so must now follow its lead. That the sinner is repeatedly transformed into ash and then reconstituted manifests the horror of chaos; it is a parody of the supra-formal. The damned soul goes through 'death' over and over, yet cannot die. To *steal* is to identify with something incompatible with one's true identity; those who do not see their own forms, or have not realized them, must grab for outer forms that do not belong to them. The phoenix is like an obsessive attempt to hold on to forms that are always dissolving in the passage of time. In the Terrestrial Paradise the Spirit is so wedded to forms and so transfigures them that it is not necessary there to experience the decay inherent in carnal existence. The phoenix is like a parody of this terrestrial incorruptibility; it is a false idea of Eternity as cyclical time, like that of the Stoic philosophers. This sinner, who 'around him looks / Wholly bewildered by the mighty anguish / Which he has suffered' is bound to the Wheel of Birth and Death.[1]

The bewildered sinner is Vanni Fucci, who is being punished for stealing sacred objects:

---

1. One could say that the phoenix and the bewildered sinner express ideas that are analogous to the Buddhist concept that manifest existence, fuelled by craving and delusion, is a round of 'reincarnational' existences, separated—and, in a sense, created—by forgetfulness, which Dante dramatizes here by comparing it to the effects of an epileptic seizure. The Buddhist idea of reincarnation is not that of an enduring self which clothes itself in a series of physical bodies; desire and ignorance simply produce, according to the law of *karma*, suffering sentient beings who have forgotten their true nature. In terms of Hinduism, René Guénon (for one) denies that the doctrine of literal reincarnation—that one human person, through a process of death and rebirth, turns into another—is in line with the Vedanta, which teaches that 'Brahman (the Absolute Godhead) is the One and Only Transmigrant.' The Shaivite rendering of this teaching might be expressed as follows: 'God forgets Who He is in order to become us (though in His inviolable Essence He never really forgets); we remember Who we are in order to become Him.' This doctrine is in some ways analogous to the Christian, patristic formulation: 'God (through Christ) becomes as we are that we might become as He is.'

'. . . *It pains me more that thou hast caught me*
  Amid this misery where thou seest me,
  Than when I from the other life was taken.
What thou demandest I cannot deny;
  So low am I put down because I robbed
  The sacristy of its fair ornaments,
And blame was falsely laid upon another;
  But lest you in the sight of me take pleasure
  If thou shalt ever emerge from these dark places,
To this prediction open your ears, and listen:
  Pistoia first will strip itself of Blacks;
  Then Florence shall renew her men and manners;
Mars will draw up a vapor from Val di Magra,
  Which turbid clouds will then try to enwrap,
  The clash between them will be fierce, impetuous.
Above Campo Picen shall be the battle;
  Then shall the vapor suddenly split the clouds,
  And every White be sorely stricken by it.
I've predicted this that it might give thee pain.' [133–151]

The theft of sacred objects involves a denial of revelation and a dependence upon human ingenuity. Vanni Fucci, in his act of 'stealing spirit,' was stealing what was already his by his human birthright as a being made in the Image of God. Spirit is given as the grace of the sacraments is given, but because he attempted to steal it, he couldn't retain what otherwise would have naturally (or supernaturally) been his, which is why he is unable now either to keep or to lose his human form. [See quote from Thomas Merton's, 'Prometheus: A Meditation', p 69.] Vanni Fucci makes his prediction only to hurt Dante; he himself derives no good from it—a fit punishment for a thief. He is so ashamed of his exposure that he strikes at Dante like a snake; this foreshadows the sins of betrayal punished in the lowest circles. Betrayal directly violates the bond of love, and Vanni Fucci's swift psychological attack has an intensity to it that is not unlike a perverted love. It employs a deep intuitive understanding of the other, but only in order to hurt; the living relationship itself is without value or significance.

Canto XXV

At the conclusion of his words, the defiant thief
  Raised his fists aloft with both figs cocked,
  Crying: 'Take that, God, for at Thee I aim them!'
From that time forth the serpents were my friends;
  For one entwined itself about his neck
  As if it said: 'Now you will speak no more';
And round his arms another, who retied them,
  Clinching itself together so in front,
  That with them he could not a motion make. [1–9]

THE THIEVES are related to those 'confidence men' who try to steal
other people's trust. The thief is a conscious hypocrite, the hypocrite an unconscious thief. In his attempt to curse God, which sets
the stage for the metamorphoses to follow, Vanni Fucci tries to use
the human form as if it were his to command, forgetting that his
very being and essence are a divine gift. His conscious rebellion
against God, the greatest so far encountered in the *Inferno*,
announces the loss of the human form made in God's Image. The
soul becomes bestial, and the beast takes on a human semblance.
There is an ironic justice in this: Vanni Fucci, who in CANTO XXIV
cursed Dante, is now silenced by the serpents after cursing God.
When Dante says 'from that time forth, those serpents were my
friends' [4], he shows that he has transcended the personal desire
for vengeance, and accepted the impartiality of Divine Justice: 'Vengeance is Mine sayeth the Lord.'

And I beheld a Centaur full of rage
  Come crying out: 'Where is he, where's that scoffer?'
I do not think Maremma has so many
  Serpents as he had all along his back,
  As far as where his human part began.
Upon the shoulders, just behind the nape,
  With wings wide open did a dragon lie,
  And he set fire to all that he encountered.
My Master said: 'That one is Cacus, who
  Within a grotto beneath Mount Aventine
  Created oftentimes a lake of blood.
He goes not on the same road with his brothers,
  By reason of the fraudulent theft he made
  From the great herd, which was near to him;
Whereat his crooked actions ceased beneath
  The club of Hercules. . . .' [17–32]

In the centaur Cacus, who is searching for Hercules his slayer, intent upon revenge, the mammalian nature is totally taken over by the reptilian one; *empathy* is completely negated. The dragon on the centaur's back is the demon that incites sinners to theft for theft's sake. He envies anyone who possesses anything at all; his desire to steal something is based purely on the fact that it belongs to someone else. This is the nature of evil: since it is a deficit of reality, it can only exist as a parasite on the True and the Good, like the *ivy* in line 58. Cacus is a lower echo of Geryon, a symbol of an even darker level of deceit; according to Greek myth, the centaur stole the cattle of Geryon from Hercules, who ultimately slew him.

As I kept my eyes fixed hard upon those sinners
  A serpent having six feet darted out
  In front of one, and fastened wholly on him.
With middle feet it bound him round the belly,
  And with the forward ones his arms it seized;
  And then it thrust its teeth through both his cheeks;
The hindermost pair it stretched upon his thighs,
  Then forced its tail in between the two,

And straightened it up along his lower back.
Ivy was never so fastened by its fibers
    Unto a tree, as this horrible reptile
    Upon the other's limbs entwined its own.
Then they stuck close, as if of heated wax
    They had been made, and intermixed their color,
    Till neither appeared as he has been before.
Just as, on burning paper, a brownish stain
    Moves upward along the page before the flame,
    Which, though white is dying, is not yet black,
The other two looked on, and each of them
    Cried out: 'Ah me, Agnello, how you've changed!
    Look! Now you are neither two nor one.'
Already the two heads had joined together,
    When in one face, in which two had been lost,
    Two intermingled shapes appeared to us.
Of the four lengths there were now composed two arms,
    And the thighs and legs, the belly and the chest
    Became such limbs as never yet were seen.
Every original aspect was cancelled there;
    In two and nothing that perverted image
    Shared. . . . [49–78]

The metamorphosis of Agnello ('lamb') is a parody of the two natures of Christ, 'Who, being in the form of God, thought it not *robbery* to be equal with God: But made himself of no reputation, and took upon him the form of a servant, and was made in the likeness of men' [Philippians 2:6–7]. As opposed to the hypostatic union of the divine and human natures in Christ, Agnello is cursed by a horrible ontological ambivalence; he is 'neither two nor one.' His condition is also a parody of true relatedness; in Agnello's case, in coming together the two entities are destroyed, not fulfilled.

The Incarnation has everything to do with the mystery of relatedness; the Divine and human natures come together without violating either their uniqueness or their union. In Dante's relationship with Beatrice, divine and human love are one because they stand in the right relationship, which is why Beatrice can appear in some sense as a type of Christ; it is because of Christ's incarnation that Dante's love for Beatrice can exist. In Agnello's metamorphosis, however, the two natures are not the Divine and the human but the human and the instinctual, as with the centaur Cacus; and when human and subhuman marry, the subhuman always rules. *Theft* in the realm of relationships appears as 'co-dependency'; personal boundaries become blurred, destroying any possibility of mutual respect, and the relationship ends in chaos: 'Every original aspect was cancelled there/In two and nothing that perverted image/ Shared. . . .' [76–78].

> *Even as a lizard, under the dog day's lash*
> > *Darting from hedge to hedge in summer heat*
> > *Appears like lightning if it cross the road,*
> *Thus did appear, streaking towards the bellies*
> > *Of the other two, a small fiery serpent,*
> > *Livid and black as is a peppercorn.*
> *And in that part wherein is first received*
> > *Our nourishment, one of them it transfixed;*
> > *Then downward fell in front of him outstretched.*
> *The one transfixed gazed upon it, speechless;*
> > *All he did was stand his ground and yawn,*
> > *Just as if sleep or fever had overcome him.*
> *He at the serpent gazed, and it at him;*
> > *One through the wound, the other through the mouth*
> > *Smoked violently, and the two smokes blended.*
> *Henceforth be silent Lucan, where you sing*
> > *Of wretched Sabellus and Nassidius,*
> > *And wait to hear what flies forth from my bow.*
> *Be silent Ovid, about Cadmus and Arethusa;*
> > *For if of him to snake, of her to fountain,*
> > *He sings the transformation, I grudge him not;*
> *Because two natures never face to face*
> > *Has he transmuted, so that both the forms*
> > *Stood ready to exchange their very matter.*
> *They responded to each other in this way:*
> > *The serpent to a fork first split his tail,*

And the wounded sinner drew his feet together.
The legs at first, and soon the thighs themselves
　　Grew so together, that in no time at all
　　Of their juncture no visible sign remained.
He with the cloven tail assumed the figure
　　The other one was losing, while his skin
　　Became elastic, and the other's hard.
I saw the arms draw inward at the armpits,
　　And both feet of the reptile, that had been short,
　　Grew by just as much as the other's shrank.
After that the snake's hind feet, together twisted,
　　Became the member that a man conceals,
　　While the other's member sprouted two similar feet.
The smoke hid both of them beneath new colors;
　　It made the hair sprout on the skin of one
　　While stripped and bald the other's skin became.
The first rose up as down the second fell,
　　Though each kept his evil lamps fixed on the other
　　Beneath which both the muzzles of them altered.
The standing one drew his in towards his temples,
　　And from excess matter which collected
　　Two ears pushed outward from the hollow cheeks;
What had not been pulled back but still remained
　　Turned most of his human face into a nose,
　　And thickened his lips, as was appropriate.
He who lay prostrate thrust his muzzle forward,
　　And backward drew his ears into his head,
　　Just like a snail pulling in its horns;
And so the tongue, that earlier had been whole
　　And fit for speech, now split—and in the other
　　The cleft tongue closed up, and the smoking stopped.
The soul, which to a reptile had been changed,
　　Along the valley hissing took its flight,
　　And after him the other spoke and spit.
Then he turned away from him his new-made shoulders
　　And told another: 'I'd have Buoso run
　　Crawling along this road as I have done.'

> *In this way I beheld the seventh ballast*
> *Shift and reshift; let strangeness be my excuse*
> *If here confusion issues from my pen.* [79–144]

The attack of the 'blazing little serpent' puts this soul—that of Cianfa—into an infernal trance, totally annihilating its capacity for spiritual attention; the sharpness and swiftness of the serpent present an inverted image of the vigilance it has destroyed. It attacks at the navel in order to draw the sinner toward what is below the human form; it does this by inverting the process by which that form originally developed. The smoke from the serpent's mouth and that from the sinner's navel meet and blend; the smoking mouth symbolizes greater awareness than does the smoking navel, and it is this awareness which gives the demon his power to dominate the sinner. The blending of the two smokes foreshadows a sub-human transformation, similar to a development which begins in the subtle or animic realm before appearing in the physical one. And this is precisely what happens when inhuman modes of being appear on the human level: the human aspect of the soul begins to seem uncouth, bestial and uncivilized, while its manipulative, bestial, subhuman aspects will start to look more human. This shows the tragedy—or rather the irony—of the attempt to base one's evaluation of others only on the personal dimension.

When Dante brags that he has surpassed Lucan and Ovid, he brags as a Christian; only someone who lives under the sign of the hypostatic union of the Divine and human natures can see what these pagan poets were really trying to get at in their half-understood stories of metamorphoses; and only a Christian can understand the depth of evil represented by their unconscious parodies of the Incarnation. Christ is true man and true God, not *part* man and *part* God like a centaur or some other mythological monster. The deepest evil, the evil of the Antichrist, will be based on just this kind of parody of the hypostatic union.

In the Platonic view, forms reside in a higher world, that of the permanent archetypes—a doctrine which is opposed to our habitual view of forms as being made up of whatever has already been concretized, already 'taken form.' This is why matter flows from form to form in the first stage of this metamorphosis, instead of one form changing into another: 'both the forms/Stood ready to exchange their very matter' [101–102]. In Aristotelian terminology, *materia* is ever-changing while *forma* is eternal. But in the second stage, each form changes into its opposite: since both the sinner and his tormenting demon have departed from their real forms, they cannot hold them. The forms themselves have not fundamentally altered; in Hell, however, they remain as eternal judgments against the souls that have refused to conform to them.

The six-legged serpent of the first metamorphosis is the symbol of a grasping possessiveness; the blazing little serpent of the second— suggesting the nimbleness of the pickpocket now become its own eternal punishment—represents the total inability to grasp what should be grasped: the human form.

When Dante speaks of the 'seventh ballast' [142], he is again having intimations of the higher worlds he is drawing closer to— specifically, the seven terraces of the *Purgatorio*. He sees the sinners of the Seventh Pouch as the *weight* necessary to keep the ship of the *Commedia* on an even keel; he grasps the necessity of Hell in light of the totality of the Divine Order.

Canto XXVI

Still the Eighth Circle, Seventh Pouch: the place of the Fraudulent Counselors. The last voyage of Ulysses.

THIS CANTO of the *Commedia* opens with Dante inveighing against the city of Florence since he has found so many of her citizens in Hell. Florence is a city proud of her ability to extend influence over land and sea, but to Dante, shame is much more appropriate for her than pride. If so many of her citizens have fallen spiritually, she can lay no claim to true honor.

Because of a visionary dream that comes to him before dawn, Dante understands that Florence is about to experience the misfortune that her enemies have hoped would overtake her, and part of Dante's soul, like his city's enemies, deeply consents to Florence's sorrowful destiny. Dante, speaking in modern psychological terms, has seen too much of his city's shadow, which is why he no longer believes the things she boastfully says about herself. He desires her downfall, even though this misfortune will be grievous to him also. Dante is a citizen of Florence, after all, and his soul is joined in many ways to her destiny, dark though it may be. Her downfall will bring upon him suffering and even exile.

Contemplating the sorrowful state of Florence causes Dante to remember that he must discipline his own talent so that it will serve the spiritual virtues, instead of setting it up as an idol or idolizing others by means of it.

What Dante witnesses next is a scene that dazzles him, a sight that might lure many a poet to write about it in such a way that it would lead his soul not toward integrity, as the virtues do, but 'beyond virtue,' toward fragmentation and destruction. He looks below and sees at the bottom of this pit many flames, each one of which has captivated the soul of a sinner. These flames remind Dante of how, in early summer, a farmer will look down from a hilltop upon a multitude of fireflies. On earth, that scene is beautiful. Thinking of it, Dante is reminded of how Elisha saw the chariot of Elijah rise ever higher toward Heaven, till its single flame became like a small cloud, ascending so far that it finally passed out of sight. The flames Dante is watching, however, are sinking below him into the pit of Hell, and if he not were holding tightly to a rock he would certainly have fallen into the pit himself.

The allusion to Elijah's chariot indicates a direct perversion of the spiritual Path, which he elaborates in his subsequent treatment of the last voyage of Ulysses. (The fiery chariot of Elijah represents a vertical ascent towards the Spirit, of which the ship of Ulysses, sailing horizontally across this world's oceans, is the mere counterfeit.)

Virgil speaks to Dante now, since he knows how easy it is for a poet to be swept away from God by the glamour of what he sees. He explains that each of these fires which so fascinate him has imprisoned at least one sinner.

When Dante looks at this scene again, his attention fixes upon one particular flame, a flame that invokes for him not the glory of the Spirit, but the image of a funeral pyre. He thinks especially of the pyre that Eteocles and Polynices were burned upon, twin brothers who bore each other such enmity in life that, after they died, the fire that consumed their corpses split into two flames.

The flame that Dante sees is also a double-headed flame. Virgil tells him that Ulysses and Diomedes now share one punishment within it. It is as if this fire were a single soul in which the intellect and the will are divided against each other. In life they had both worked for a Greek victory over Troy, but they could only achieve this victory through fraud and violence. Both methods, while they may bring success, also breed continuing enmity and treachery. Not only did Ulysses and Diomedes build the Trojan horse—a false gift if there ever was one—but they also stole the statue of Pallas Athene, protectress of Troy. Nothing was sacred to them.

Dante implores Virgil to be allowed to speak to these souls. Virgil replies that while he admires this impulse, it would be better if he himself spoke to them. These are the souls of ancient Greeks, and it is more likely that Virgil, who lived in classical antiquity, will be well received; furthermore, they might be disdainful of Dante's speech.

When Virgil addresses the Greeks, he reminds them of how they were mentioned in his great poem, the *Aeneid*. Of course these souls cannot have the everlasting life that Christian hope for; they do, however, possess the kind of immortality that memory and history may give. But they cannot see how history itself is a contingent thing which turns to dust when confronted with the eternity of God.

When asked what brought about their deaths, Ulysses replies, speaking in terms of that lesser immortality he does understand. In describing his death, he also recounts how his soul went astray.

Ulysses was a cunning man—which is why, though seduced by Circe and transformed into a swine, he was eventually able to escape. If Circe could turn his soul into that of a pig, it meant that she could capture his attention and draw it so far down into his animal nature that it could no longer recognize its own human qualities, such as rationality and compassion.

As recounted in the *Odyssey*, Ulysses finally broke away from the attraction of Circe and returned home to Ithaca—but he did not save his soul. He saw that it was his duty to love his son and his old father, and that nothing in this world would more please his wife Penelope than his staying with her until the end of their lives. She, after all, had waited faithfully for him, weaving during the day and unraveling the cloth by night, while numerous suitors tried to impose their will upon her. Ulysses, who has seen so much of the world and experienced an exoticism few men ever know, feels he still needs more such experience if he is to truly understand human character. His real call, which would have saved his soul, was to stay home after all his wars and voyages. Instead, he gathers his old shipmates together, and sails west. He goes 'beyond the Sun', ever further into experience and worldliness—but after Ulysses' legendary experience of the ways of the world, what more could he possibly have needed?

Since Dante is a Christian, he looks to Christ as his Sun, as if there were no other light—and so the world 'beyond the Sun' is also beyond Christ, and ultimately beyond love; it is the 'outer darkness'.[1]

---

1. It is interesting to note that the Sun is a symbol of Christ for Muslim Sufis as well as for Christians.

Ulysses and his men set sail past the Pillars of Hercules, the Straits of Gibraltar. It is as if they believe that they can concretely sail away from contradictions like good and evil, life and death, time and eternity, the 'pairs-of-opposites' symbolized by the Pillars. These are the paradoxes that true contemplatives wrestle with in spiritual combat.

Just after passing through the Pillars of Hercules, Ulysses makes a speech to his followers, asking them to follow him 'beyond the Sun' and into an 'unpeopled world'. He never asks himself whether that world might be unpeopled because human life cannot subsist there without grave imbalances to the soul.[2] He tells his men that since they have had the courage to travel this far west, they owe it to themselves to seek real worth and knowledge, and not live as brutes. (One is irresistibly reminded of another speech made to a ship full of westward-bound sailors by one Christopher Columbus.)

It is here that Ulysses acts as a false spiritual teacher. When he speaks to his men about 'the seed that gave you birth,' he is describing the real possibilities of spiritual development that lie hidden in human nature; and his men do indeed possess the courage and capacity to follow them through and realize them. Ulysses, however, takes his followers in exactly the wrong direction.

With great enthusiasm they resume their journey by turning their 'stern toward the morning'. The Sun, the East, the source of spiritual illumination, is now behind them. And after traveling west, they begin to veer south, toward 'the other pole and all its stars'—a false, inverted center surrounded by alienated aspects of the soul. In order to do this, they must move always toward the 'left-hand side', which in the language of the Gospels is not the way of the redeemed Sheep, but of the Goats, the reprobate. This left-hand voyaging means that at night, while they can see the other stars, they can no longer see the star of their own destiny. As that 'star of ours' has fallen below the horizon, their souls will ultimately sink into Hell.

---

2. Compare Frithjof Schuon, *Understanding Islam* (Baltimore: Penguin Books, 1972), p84, n1, where he speaks of the disequilibrium of the soul likely to result from moon travel, comparing it to *lunacy* and death. 'In all these instances,' he writes, 'the normal limits of human surroundings are outpassed. . . .'

Ulysses is blind to his own particular star, his soul's destiny, as well as to the life-circumstances that would nurture his soul unto salvation; all this has fallen below the horizon of his consciousness. When Dante describes the damned souls of the Eighth Circle moving like fireflies, they remind one of stars in the abyss below; gazing at them, he nearly falls. Just so Ulysses, having abandoned the star of his destiny so that it leaves his consciousness and sinks below the ocean's surface, is drawn after it, and damned. (When spiritual Guidance is repressed, it still attracts—but darkly.)

Dante describes Ulysses' journey as taking him toward the South Pole; the modern reader, however, cannot help but see in this south-westerly course the voyages of the great explorers and conquistadors that were yet to be. There is such an uncanny similarity between these men and the Ulysses of the *Commedia* that it is easy to imagine him sailing toward South America.

In their explorations of the New World, the conquistadors looked for fantastic places like El Dorado, the Fountain of Youth and the Seven Cities of Cibola (which remind one of the seven terraces of Purgatory); the spiritual potential that they had left behind would haunt them in a different form. In abandoning the Sun that is Christ, its own particular star, European civilization began to lose the vertical dimension, the hierarchy of being of which *The Divine Comedy* is itself the image. Consequently its spiritual potential began to move in a horizontal direction, leading to the worship of history, progress and evolution; this is what must happen when spiritual realities are seen in materialistic terms.

Sometimes the conquistadors knew that they were lost. There is a story that Pedro de Alvarado, the conqueror of Guatemala, on his deathbed kept repeating, 'I have lost my soul.' Ultimately they too, like Ulysses, had left the Sun behind—and Christ as well. When Europe discovered the New World she became richer than before, and was able to colonize places she once never new existed, and spread the Christian faith. None of this healed her, however, of the worldliness Dante laments in the *Commedia*; she moved further and further away from her own spiritual truth.

Ulysses and his men travel so far that they come upon the Mount of Purgatory. As soon as they see it they fall in love with it—but it destroys them, because they have left love and the Sun far behind. The vertical dimension, the very spiritual Path they have neglected, rises before them. They see it, but they cannot land on its shores. A whirlwind comes up out of that new land which Dante calls *la nova tierra*—reminding us once again of the New World yet to be discovered—and beats against the ship until it lifts up its stern. That same stern that Ulysses has turned against the morning and against the Spirit that might have saved them is now ironically exalted. They have met the Divine, but met it as an alien reality. Their ship sinks, and the sea covers them with its darkness.

✠

Critics often say that here in the CANTO XXVI of the *Inferno*, Dante intuits the beauty and grandeur of the nascent Renaissance; they believe that the poet's portrayal of Ulysses shows him as noble and courageous, though damned. But isn't this Canto really a criticism on Dante's part of things we would otherwise unthinkingly see as noble, since we fail to see them in the light of spiritual truth? The soul of Ulysses, after all, is not in Purgatory; it isn't even in the Limbo of the righteous pagans; it is eternally damned in the Eighth Circle of Hell.

In this context it is not insignificant that Dante prays that his talent not exceed the bounds of virtue—for if it did, if he were to take the story of Ulysses on the level of foolish hero-worship and forget that this hero is damned, he would do us a great disservice. Ulysses, too, went 'beyond virtue', and in so doing departed from his star, his guidance. It is part of Dante's greatness that he was able to show us how the seemingly heroic voyage of Ulysses, which Dante clearly admires on certain levels, was actually the ultimate defeat.

Canto XXVII

Still the Seventh Pouch of the Eighth Circle, hell of the Fraudulent Counselors. Guido da Montefeltro and The damnation of Pope Boniface VIII. The punishment of the Antinomians.

> *Already was the flame erect and silent,*
> *It had no more to say, and now departed*
> *With the permission of the gentle Poet;*
> *When yet another, which behind it came,*
> *Caused us to turn and gaze upon its tip*
> *By a confused sound that issued from it.*
> *As that Sicilian bull (who bellowed first*
> *With cry of him—such punishment was just—*
> *Who had shaped it with his instruments)*
> *Bellowed so with the voice of the afflicted,*
> *That, notwithstanding it was made of brass,*
> *It still appeared with agony transfixed;*
> *Having found no path or exit from the flame*
> *Since their first moment, those despairing words*
> *Were changed into the language of the fire. [1–15]*

THE BULL OF PHALARIS—a brazen bull which was heated like a furnace in order to kill those imprisoned within it, so that their screams of pain would sound like the roaring of the bull—symbolizes intelligence (the fire) totally separated from compassion (for the victim), which involves the attempt to pervert intelligence itself —as, for example, in the case of certain cunning and unscrupulous lawyers.[1] The one who fashioned it (the craftsman Perillus) was the

---

1. This is St. Augustine's definition of demonic intelligence in *The City of God*.

first to be roasted inside it: intelligence without love turns on itself, destroys itself. Like the Bull which conceals its victim, here the flame itself appears to suffer, whereas the suffering is really that of the sinner imprisoned within it. Those who employ lies and cunning seem to possess the power to distort intelligence itself—yet the spiritual Intellect, here symbolized by the flame, in its essence can never be corrupted. As James Cutsinger points out:

> The Intellect or intuitive power remains infallible, and its knowledge is in need of nothing, even virtuous living . . . knowledge is its own proof and guarantee. Nevertheless 'man is not the Intellect.' Uncreated and uncreatable, the Intellect is greater than he is. If he means to assimilate what the Intellect shows him, his individuality must be modified and brought into line.[2]

That the words of the sinner had been 'transformed into the language of the fire' [15] demonstrates that, by the power and justice of God, even lies are made to serve the truth.

Next Dante speaks with the soul of Guido da Montefeltro, who gave evil counsel to Pope Boniface VIII after the pope falsely absolved him of the sin he was *about* to commit:

> *'While I was still the form of bone and pulp*
> *My mother gave to me, the deeds I did*
> *Were not those of a lion, but a fox.'* [73–75]

Guido reminds us here that all terrestrial life takes place within the realm of the *prima materia* or Universal Nature (the Great Mother), which is also the realm of *maya*.

> *'When now unto that portion of mine age*
> *I saw myself arrived, when each one ought*
> *To lower the sails, and coil away the ropes,*
> *That which before had pleased me, now displeased;*
> *Confessed and penitent I renounced the world*

---

2. *Advice to the Serious Seeker: Meditations on the Teaching of Frithjof Schuon*, (Albany: SUNY Albany, 1997), p59.

Ah woe is me! It should have done me good.
The Leader of the modern Pharisees. . . . [79–85]
Asked me for advice, but I was silent,
    Because his words appeared so wild and drunk.
And then he said: "Be not thy heart afraid;
    Henceforth I thee absolve, so now instruct me
    How to raze Palestrina to the ground. . . ." [98–102]
Then with weighty arguments he urged me on
    Until silence seemed a greater sin than speech;
    Till I said: "Father, since thou washest me
Of that sin into which I now must fall:
    Make promise long and its fulfilment short;
    That's how you'll triumph on your lofty throne."' [106–111]

Guido da Montefeltro tried to save his soul by craft, and so lost sight of the crucial role of basic *intent*, which always takes precedence over the form of the act;[3] he erred in believing that the outer form of Pope Boniface's act of absolution carried greater weight than the intent behind it. Yet his acceptance of false absolution from Boniface—which was only a semblance of the outer form, since to

---

3. It was this truth which led Meister Eckhart to assert that there are no intrinsically evil acts, a principle which is also illustrated in *Sura al-Kahf* of the Koran, where Moses encounters a spiritual master, identified by the Sufis with the immortal prophet Khidr, their invisible patron, whose acts seem evil and shocking until the intent behind them is explained. Such apparent antinomianism is not intended to abrogate the law, however: in order to meet Khidr, you first have to be Moses. In the words of Jesus, 'Think not I am come to destroy the law, or the prophets: I am not come to destroy, but to fulfil' [Matt. 5:17] The great Sufi metaphysician Ibn al-'Arabi, who himself received teachings from al-Khidr—and who, according to Miguel Asín y Palacios, was the source for much of the material drawn upon by Dante for his *Commedia*—has this to say about the error of antinomianism: 'Beware lest you throw the Scale of the Law from your hand in exoteric knowledge (*al-'ilm as-rasmi*) and in accomplishing what it sets down in its rulings. If you understand from it something different than what the people understand, such that your understanding comes between you and the performance of the outward significance (*zahir*) of its rulings, then do not rely upon your understanding! For it is a deception of the ego (*makr nafsi*) in a divine form without your being aware.' [William Chittick, *The Sufi Path of Knowledge: Ibn al-'Arabi's Metaphysics of the Imagination*, (Albany: SUNY Press, 1989), p257.

pretend to absolve someone of a sin he has not yet committed is a
violation of the form as well as an indication of perverted intent—
opened him to the opposite error: the belief that the elect who have
been justified by grace cannot sin, no matter what acts they
commit—the error of *antinomianism*. It is as if Guido were asking
the law to put him above the law.[4]

Guido was close to the spiritual influence of St. Francis; he sin-
cerely tried to repent by joining the Franciscan Order; his sincerity
perhaps mirrored by the repentance of his son Buonconte at the
moment of death, as recounted in the fifth Canto of the *Purgatorio*.
Guido was close to goodness, but at the last minute evil overtook
him; Buonconte was close to darkness, but at the last minute Grace
triumphed in his soul.

Guido was unconscious of his core intent, and so gave himself
false counsel. If someone can be unconscious of his own real intent
to this degree, even less can *we* presume to divine it. Guido himself
would probably have considered the spiritual influence of St. Francis to be an expression of his own deepest intent, and have looked
upon all these political maneuvers as merely the outer layer of his
soul, unrelated to his eternal destiny. He undoubtedly believed this
because the grace of St. Francis, in and of itself, *was* on a higher
level than his political activity—and yet the center of his will was in
fact fixed on politics and not on grace.

> '*If I believed that my reply were made*
> *To one who to the world would ever return,*
> *This flame without more flickering would stand still;*
> *But inasmuch as never from this depth*
> *Did any one return, if I hear true,*
> *Without the fear of infamy I answer. . . .*' [61–66]

---

4. Since Christians are justified by the grace of Christ's atonement and not by
the Torah, antinomianism is a perennial temptation. True, St. Paul said that 'Christ
hath redeemed us from the curse of the law' (Gal. 3:13); but he also said 'No whore-
monger, nor unclean person, nor covetous man, who is an idolater, hath any inher-
itance in the kingdom of Christ and of God' (Eph. 5:5).

Here Guido accepts the general, received wisdom about the nature of Hell, and thus fails to see Dante's *particular* reality—specifically, the fact that he is alive. To accept and follow received wisdom entails inescapable obligations, which Guido did not fulfill; consequently he remains bound in the afterlife to this same level of general ideas, of *hearsay*; he is unable to see beyond this level to the actual thing itself.

> *'But even as Constantine sought out Sylvester*
> *To cure his leprosy, upon Soracte,*
> *So this one sought me out as an adept*
> *To cure him of the fever of his pride.'* [94–97]

Pope Boniface VIII is compared with Constantine because, as opposed to his predecessor, Celestine V, he sought the wrong kind of power: imperial rather than sacerdotal. It was Boniface who, in the papal bull *Unam Sanctam*, asserted that 'to be subject to the pope is, for all human creatures, a necessity of salvation.'

> *'Heaven have I power to lock and to unlock,*
> *As thou dost know; therefore the keys are two,*
> *The which my predecessor held not dear.'* [103–105]

Boniface's 'predecessor' was Pope Celestine V. In *Esoterism as Principle and as Way*, pp162–167, Frithjof Schuon tells the story of Celestine and Boniface, and explains Dante's particular response to them as expressed in *The Divine Comedy*. Since these passages go a long way toward placing Dante in his proper historical, political and spiritual contexts, they are worth quoting at length:

One of the contradictions, real or apparent, to be found in the Divine Comedy is the fact that Dante places in hell a saint, namely Pope Celestine V, whom the poet reproaches for having abdicated and for having thus betrayed his charge. Here is the story, one that is well known but inevitably lost sight of by many people: the holy see having remained vacant for over two years—following the death of Nicholas IV towards the end of the 13th century—the cardinals elected the hermit Pier Angelerio from Murhonne in the Abruzzi, an aged holy man who had founded the Celestine order; the reason for this unexpected election is that the hermit had threatened them with hell-fire if they delayed any longer in electing a pope. From the moment of his election, the holy man—who took the name of Celestine V—was held more or less prisoner in Naples by King Charles II and the Colonna clan, protagonists of the moral and political reform of Christianity. The new pope soon proceeded to nominate some cardinals of the same tendency, which was the only thing to do, but which aroused lively protests from the opposing 'worldly' party, represented especially by the Caetani clan; and it was a cardinal of this family who entreated the pope to abdicate in his favor and who, having become pope in his turn—under the name of Boniface VIII—held his predecessor prisoner in Rome; it was there that Celestine died after two years of captivity.

In the first passage of the *Inferno* that refers to Celestine V, Dante 'sees and recognizes' in the first circle of hell, reserved for the sins of omission, 'the shadow of him who from cowardice (*per vita*) made the great refusal' (iii, 58–60); while in a third passage, it is Boniface himself who is reproached for 'having taken the Beautiful Lady (the Church) by fraud (from Celestine), and thereafter having abused her' (xix, 55–57). Dante's attitude toward Celestine V may appear exaggerated, but one must take into account the following factors: firstly, the canonization of the hermit pope, which was promulgated in the pontificate of Clement V, took place, as far as one can tell, after the completion of the *Inferno*; secondly, Dante avoids mentioning Celestine V by name, and some have even supposed that in the first passage Dante is speaking, not of this pope, but of Esau or Diocletian, both of them more or less traitors to their charge; finally, only this first passage places the pope in hell—granting that in fact it is the pope who is referred to—while the other two passages place Boniface VIII in hell, and the allusions to Celestine V— incontestable in these instances—do not imply that he too is damned.

Be that as it may, if Dante did not hesitate to make the insinuations just mentioned, this can be explained by considerations of both a spiritual and political nature which were to the discredit of Boniface VIII, and also, from another point of view, by the haughty and combative nature of the poet; the election of Boniface was made possible only by Celestine's abdication, an unprecedented act in the history of the papacy. The hermit-pope has been reproached for having fallen, without resistance, under the influence of the Colonnas—a reproach which is in no wise conclusive, for the Colonnas were on the side of the *spirituali,* and, like the pope, hated the ambitions and insatiable worldliness of the clergy; Celestine V had no motive, to say the least, for opposing just tendencies which were in conformity with his own sentiments, merely because his quasi-jailers also subscribed to them.

Celestine V could in principle have achieved these plans for the renewal of the Church, but he quickly came up against unexpected difficulties of a kind largely unimaginable for a man of his sort; it was for having missed this opportunity, and having missed it in favor of one of the chief representatives of the worldly tendency, that Dante could not forgive him.

It remains to be explained why Celestine V, a virtuous man if there ever was one, shrank from what Dante considered to be an imperative duty; the reasons for his having done so had no interest for the eagle of Florence, or at least they escaped him at the moment of writing the Inferno, but they do explain and excuse the attitude of the holy pontiff, who a priori was hardly a man of this low world. By this we mean that he was a born contemplative, that is to say a contemplative not by conversion but by nature.

In the language of gnosis, he was called a 'pneumatic', namely a being who is attracted to Heaven in a 'supernaturally natural' manner; the name Celestinus, chosen by the new pope and given to the monastic order which he founded, is also an indication of this. The 'pneumatic' lives on the memory of a lost paradise: he seeks only one thing, a return to his origin, and having himself a quasi-angelic nature, he is to a large extent unaware of the average nature of men. Incapable of knowing in advance that the general run of men are wild beasts, Celestine V, with a holy naivety, believed them to be similar to—or even better than— himself; he was unaware to what extent passions, ambitions and other illusions dominate intelligences and wills, and to what extent men are capable of pretense—which incidentally proves their culpability. He had to become pope to find this out. . . .

Pier Angelerio accepted the tiara because he believed that this was the will of God; but what Providence wanted for him was a spiritual experience and not the pontificate; an experience which was at the same time an instruction for others in incorruptibility and not an example of weakness, still less of cowardice. God also wished to show that there are vocations that are mutually exclusive—in the absence of very rare gifts, to be found above all in Prophets—and that no vocation is more pleasing to him than that of contemplation, which includes all the others in a potential manner. Moreover, Celestine V would have been an ideal pope in the normal ambience that Dante wished for, that is to say, under the protection of a powerful emperor fully conscious of his charge, and consequently freed from the political interferences with which the Roman pontiffs had to contend; it was undoubtedly from the normal point of view that the hermit from the Arbuzzi accepted the tiara and it was because of the same point of view that the Florentine poet did not forgive him for having renounced it. The whole problem here lies in the definition of 'duty': the imprescriptible vocation of the contemplative—of the 'pneumatic' whose spiritual ascent results from his very substance and not from a choice or a conversion as in the case of the 'psychic'—may possibly be reconcilable with activity in the world, but there are cases—and this is more probable—where it is not so. At all events, it is through the duties that are properly his that the contemplative fully satisfies the love of God, and thereby the love of men, the latter being contained in the former.

Dante's intention was to replace the illegitimate worldliness of the popes with the legitimate status of the emperors, this lay status being entirely relative and in a certain manner a priesthood in its turn. Celestine was the very type of a spiritual pope; it was certainly not a pontiff of his sort who would have favored the worldly and humanist revolution of the Renaissance, and thus inaugurated the self-destruction of Christianity. Naturally Dante could not foresee the nature of the cultural revolution of the Medicis and the Borgias, but he discerned its principle; he could see far-off consequences in nearby causes. The state of urgency, he thought, did not permit considerations of personal vocation, even in the case of a saint like Celestine V.

What Dante foresaw, his contemporaries did not know or did not want to know; the incorrigible brawlers of the Middle Ages imagined they could kill and plunder each other indefinitely in the name of God and the angels and the saints; they lacked the presentiment that this very contradiction, if it went beyond certain limits, would culminate in the destruction of their supremacy and their form of government, and at the same time of Western Christendom. Dante had been called a 'dreamer' because his plan for the empire was never realized; if this were justified, every man who counsels wisdom and prudence is retrospectively a dreamer if he is not obeyed; and as no sage is ever fully obeyed, every sage would be a dreamer. If the norm is a dream, it is certainly no dishonor to dream.

There was not—and could not be—a between Dante and Celestine V any objective divergence on the subject of the true remedy for the evils of this world here below; but there was a subjective divergence of temperament and vocation, in the sense that Dante, while knowing perfectly the rights of pure contemplativity, thought himself unable to allow the saintly pope the benefit of these rights, and for the reasons of 'devoir d'état'. Be this as it may, in order to maintain the world in equilibrium, or even in order to improve it in a particular sector, it is not enough that there should be men capable of taking effective measures in accordance with spiritual principles, it is also necessary that there should be saints who like the 'motionless mover' of Aristotle, realize only the 'one thing necessary', namely that which constitutes the raison d'être of every human city. The sap of human 'usefulness' is the Divine 'uselessness'; this idea evokes the whole mystery of sacrifice, and above all that of the sacred in itself; of the sacred that determines all measures and at the same time escapes all measures.[5]

> '*Francis came afterward, when I was dead* [Guido continues],
>   *To take me; but one of the black Cherubim*
>   *Said "Lest you cheat me, lay no claim on him;*
> *He must come down among my chosen slaves,*
>   *Because he gave that fraudulent advice;*
>   *From that day on I've been grabbing for his hair.*
> *No-one can be absolved without repentance,*
>   *Nor can someone both repent and sin at once;*
>   *The rule of contradiction won't allow it."*
> *O miserable self! How then did I shudder*
>   *When he laid hands on me, and then cried out:*
>   *"Perhaps you thought I'd never studied logic!"*
> *He carried me on to Minos, who entwined*
>   *His tail eight times around his stubborn back,*
>   *And after he had bitten it in his rage,*
> *Said, "Here's a sinner for the thieving fire!"*' [112–127]

There can obviously be no forgiveness, no absolution, without repentance. Boniface's perversion of the meaning of scripture, which is the source of Guido's sin, is discoverable by 'mere' logic, without necessary recourse to the *gnosis* of higher realities; and this shows the validity and importance of logic on its own level.[6] Though it certainly does not do so in all cases, logic here represents

5. *Esoterism as Principle and as Way*, (Ghent, NY: Sophia Perennis, 1981), pp162–167.

6. Frithjof Schuon, in *Logic and Transcendence* (NY: Harper and Row, 1975), has the following to say about logic: 'Reason ... to the extent that it is artificially

a saving objectivity—which, because Guido has perverted it, must now argue for his damnation. Even though the 'black Cherubim', Guido's accuser, is lower ontologically than the Franciscan grace, his logic is sound—and so the accuser wins the case. (According to the *Philokalia*, the Devil, who tempts a soul to a particular sin, also acts as that soul's accuser after death [Cf. John of Karpathos, 'For the Encouragement of the Monks in India who had Written to Him: One Hundred Texts,' texts 25 and 51, *The Philokalia*, Volume One].[7]

Minos is a judge, the judge of the dead. Guido da Montefeltro is the only soul in the *Inferno* who describes his actual encounter with him, an encounter that reveals something about the quality of judgment itself. As opposed to the self-serving partiality of Guido's lawyer-like soul, Minos represents the impartiality of Divine Justice.

divorced from the Intellect, engenders individualism and arbitrariness.' (p34) 'Theology to be sure is far from disdaining the assistance of logic; it could never fall into rationalism purely and simply, however, since it is based on Revelation.' (p50)

7. The *cherubim*, the next-to-highest class of angels according to Dionysius the Areopagite in *The Celestial Hierarchy*, are sometimes represented as wheels studded with eyes, in line with Ezekiel's vision of God's Throne [Eze. 1:18; 10:2], symbolizing the spiritual Intellect which can look in all directions simultaneously. The 'black Cherubim' thus indicates a satanic inversion of this Intellect, which is what logic becomes when it attempts to act on its own, unguided by Intellectual intuition.

Canto XXVIII

Eighth Circle, Ninth Pouch, the Sowers of Schism and Scandal.
Mohammed and Ali. Curio. Bertran de Born.

THESE SOULS tried to gain by creating conflicts that other people would have to live with; they believed that peace can be established by exporting war. But to distance oneself from conflict by trying to impose it upon others is in no way peace. True peace is based upon integration: if seemingly opposed realities such as love and knowledge, reason and intuition, intellect and will are united within the soul, this in turn makes unity possible on the level of human relationships. To the integrated soul, individual differences are complementary, not mutually exclusive; they lead to relationship rather than conflict.

> *A barrel that's lost its end-piece or its hoop*
>   *Was never shattered so, as the one I saw*
>   *Ripped from the chin to where one breaketh wind.*
> *Between his legs were hanging down his entrails;*
>   *His heart was visible, and the dismal sack*
>   *That maketh excrement of what is eaten.*
> *While I was all absorbed in seeing him,*
>   *He looked at me, and opened with his hands*
>   *His bosom, saying: 'See now how I split myself;*
> *How mutilated, see, is poor Muhammad;*
>   *In front of me doth Ali weeping go,*
>   *His face split open from forelock down to chin;*
> *And all the others whom thou seest here*
>   *Disseminators of scandal and of schism*
>   *While living were, and therefore so are split.*
> *A devil is behind us here, who cleaves us*

> *Thus cruelly, putting to the sabre's edge*
> *Each one of this whole throng yet once again,*
> *Each time we have gone around the doleful road;*
> *He does this because our wounds have closed again*
> *Before any pass in front of him once more.'*[1] [22–42]

To cause dissension splits the soul—which is why Mohammed terms the sowing of scandal 'self-accusation' [45]—and a split soul is always causing dissension. Thus the work of self-integration, while usually not identified with peacemaking, is not ultimately selfish; it serves a real social function. To overcome the inner divisions of the soul is also to overcome *shame*: there is nothing more conducive to shame than unconscious self-sabotage, and nothing more productive of conflict than unconscious shame.

The figure of Mohammed here relates to the collective psychic pain produced by the crusades, a pain we are still living with in many ways today, though Dante would not have seen the Christian hand in this suffering as well as we might. The endless circling of the souls of Mohammed and Ali is like an addiction to conflict, a failure to reach integration of soul. The split torso of Mohammed and the split head of Ali suggest the attempt to make one's way through life by creating and benefiting from conflicts that reach beyond oneself to others, though their original cause lies within one's soul. The *ring* is a symbol of integrity; the wedding ring, for example, symbolizes faithfulness and constancy. But to endlessly walk around in a ring is only a parody of this integrity. Psychic integration has been discarded by these souls; they have entered the 'vicious cycle' of conflict. The piling up of discarded rings after a battle [11], and the image of the barrel losing its hoops [22] are symbols of this loss of integration. These souls must act out a repetitive

---

1. Dante's image of Ali and Mohammed seems to be based upon the *ahadith*. Ali in fact died after being struck in the face with a poisoned sword; and when Mohammed was a boy, according to Islamic tradition, he was approached by two men—actually angels—who opened his chest, removed his heart, washed it in a bowl of snow, and then replaced it. Dante's pairing of Ali and Mohammed in this way is like a distorted version of the *hadith* in which Mohammed declares that 'I am the city of wisdom [the torso—i.e., the heart] and Ali [the head] is its gate.'

fate because they have no detachment, no ability to stand apart from their circumstances and see them whole. In Mohammed, the root of life (the heart) is cut off, while the head still functions; Ali is wounded in the head because he is trying to follow and depend upon a heartless Mohammed. His wound is based on an attempt to perform the functions of the heart—primarily, spiritual intuition; secondarily, emotional understanding—with the head alone. A lack of heart, both as Love and as complete Intelligence, produces a divided mind. Our own excessively cerebral 'information' culture is based on the same imbalance.

> *He looked at me, and opened with his hands*
> *His bosom, saying: 'See now how I split myself. . . .'* [30–31]

Here Mohammed speaks in self-accusation, he 'spills his guts.' To create dissension in the community results in self-division; to divide others is ultimately to turn upon oneself.

A sinner named Pier da Medicina mentions the tyrant Malatestino, 'that traitor who sees only with one eye' [85], who called two nobles of Fano to a meeting at a coastal town and had them thrown overboard on the way. To see with only one eye represents a refusal of integrated knowledge and an attachment to partial knowledge, to 'partiality' and conflict.[2]

Pier da Medecina points out Caius Curio, who betrayed Pompey to Caesar for a bribe:

> *O how bewildered unto me appeared,*
> *With tongue slit asunder in his windpipe,*
> *Curio, who in speaking was so bold!* [100–102]

The split tongue of this sinner creates conflict because it can express

---

2. This is the quality represented in Islamic tradition by *al-Dajjal*, the Antichrist, who will be blind in one eye; it is the exact opposite of the sense of *unified vision* Christ was referring to when he said 'If thine eye be single, thy whole body will be full of light' [Matt. 6:22]. Christ's 'single eye' and the 'third eye' of Hinduism have substantially the same meaning.

only illusion. To speak with a forked tongue is to pervert the inherent subtlety of language, letting loose the sort of unconscious contradictions that can produce only violence. Someone who employs language in this way can say the same words to two different people and have them hear two entirely different things. The effect of this kind of speech is the exact opposite of the effect of a spiritual fable, which integrates the scattered psyche by drawing many meanings into one—as did the preaching of the Apostles on Pentecost. Though their words were heard in many different languages, in every case the inner meaning was the same.

Next Dante encounters a more formidable figure: Bertran de Born:

> *And saw a thing which I should be afraid,*
> *Without some further proof, even to recount,*
> *If it were not that conscience reassures me,*
> *That good companion which emboldens man*
> *Beneath the breastplate of its purity.* [113–117]

Dante's lesser ego-identity, his cerebral consciousness, could not have withstood the vision he is about to see of Bertran de Born carrying his own severed head; it could not have witnessed this terrible split in identity without becoming split itself. But his *conscience* can withstand it, because conscience is one aspect of the unified consciousness of the Heart.[3]

---

3. Conscience in this sense was called by the Church Fathers and the scholastic philosophers *synderesis*, defined as the innate power of the soul to know the good and discriminate between good and evil on a level higher than the rational mind. Albertus Magnus, in his *Summa Theologiae*, maintains that synderesis is possessed even by the damned, citing St. Jerome to the effect that 'this is the conscience spoken of in Prov. 18:3, "The wicked man, when he is come unto the depth of sins, contemneth, but ignominy and reproach follow him", and quoting in the same context *Isaiah* 66:24, "Their worm shall not die."' [Cf. Rama Coomaraswamy, 'The Synderesis, Commentaries by St. Albertus Magnus and Dom M. Prummer, translated from the Latin' in *The Religion of the Heart: Essays Presented to Frithjof Schuon on his Eightieth Birthday*. (Washington, DC: Foundation for Traditional Studies, 1991.]

I truly saw, and still I seem to see it,
  A trunk without a head walk in like manner
  As walked the others of the mournful herd.
And by the hair it held its severed head,
  Hung from its hand as if it were a lantern,
  A thing that gazed at us and said: 'Ah me!'
Of itself it had made itself a lamp,
  And they were two in one, and one in two;
  How that can be, He knows who so ordains it.
When it was come close to the bridge's foot,
  It lifted high the arm that held its head,
  So as to hold its words more closely toward us,
Which were: 'Behold this terrible penalty,
  Thou who, still breathing, goes forth to view the dead;
  Behold if any pain be great as this.
And so that thou may carry news of me,
  Know that am I Bertran de Born, the same
  Who gave evil encouragement to the youthful king.
Father and son I turned against each other;
  Achitophel's evil nudgings did no more
  To sow discord between Absolom and David.
Because I parted those at first so joined,
  Alas, do I now bear my brain disseered
  From its true source, which in this torso lies:
In me you see the counterstep of justice.' [118–142]

Bertran de Born, the most worldly, cynical and violent of the troubadour poets, presents the parody of a united soul, as the other sinners do not. The others, though wounded, are still relatively whole, but he is completely divided. He holds his head like a lantern, which gives the impression that he possesses a certain degree of illumination, though this is not in fact the case. The 'independence' of his head indicates a suppleness of mind that is basically meaningless and without practical effect because his head is not connected to his trunk; the mind is severed from the will, the thinking ability cut off from the faculty of Intellection residing in the spiritual Heart. And this is what makes him a perfect symbol of that tyranny of abstract thought upon which our technological society is based. Modern 'intelligence' is vast in scope and seems able to handle an immense amount of information—but on a day-to-day level, people are so distracted and inundated with information that they can't actually think. Political life—among many other things—is dying in modern societies because there is no longer any such thing as 'common sense'.

> *Of itself it had made itself a lamp,*
> *And they were two in one, and one in two. . . .* [124–125]

Although head and Heart are polarized on a certain level, they are also mysteriously one. Here, however, they are entirely at odds. That head and Heart are 'one in two' is represented by the split between the trunk and the head; that they are 'two in one' means that the head seems to be a unity in its own right, as if it were still attached to the trunk—or rather, as if the head could somehow contain the Heart, which is an impossibility. Those who try to see by the light of the ego—the head alone—are lost.

> *'Know that am I Bertran de Born, the same*
> *Who gave evil encouragement to the youthful king'.* [134–136]

Here the 'youthful king' is another reflection of the head—the offspring of the 'father', the Heart, which is its source. To 'give evil encouragement [Mandelbaum has 'give bad counsel'] so as to turn father and son against each other' is to separate cerebral consciousness from cardiac consciousness, and set them at war.

Dante's portrayal of Ali and the Prophet Mohammed as tormented sinners is deeply shocking to many Muslims, just as the Muslim denial of the Incarnation and the divine sonship of Jesus Christ is shocking to Christians. Frithjof Schuon, himself a Muslim, has this to say[4] about such contradictions, in his chapter 'The Idea of 'The Best' in Religions', from *Christianity/Islam: Essays in Esoteric Ecumenism*:

---

4. *Christianity/Islam: Essays in Esoteric Ecumenism* (Bloomington, IN: World Wisdom Books, 1985), pp 151–152.

Every religion by definition wants to be the best, and 'must want' to be the best, as a whole and also as regard to its constituent elements; this is only natural, so to speak, or rather 'supernaturally natural'.

To say form is to say exclusion of possibilities, whence the necessity for those excluded to become realized in other forms; form, since it 'excludes' by definition, is condemned to repeat itself. The contradiction between a contingent recipient and a quasi-absolute content could not be peculiar to religions alone, and in fact it is prefigured in nature: more than once we have had occasion to mention the paradoxical plurality of subjectivity within the order of conscious creatures. Individuals exclude each other because none of them can be the other, and they are opposed to one another because subjectivity by its nature is one – empirically and logically there can be only one 'I' – although we are obliged to acknowledge the mysterious evidence of subjectivity repeating itself outside ourselves and endlessly.

As every religion corresponds to a 'divine subjectivity'—or to a 'theophanic individuality'—it cannot be expected of any religion that it be 'objective' with regard to another, at least not *a priori* or exoterically; for a religion as such—as a form, precisely—the data of other religions are scarcely more than symbols or points of reference which can be used—most often in a pejorative or negative sense—within its own imagery and in accordance with its characteristic perspective.[5]

---

5. In real life the prophet Mohammed was known for his ability to reconcile warring parties and end feuds. The tribes of the oasis of Yathrib, which was later named Medina, the City of the Prophet, invited him to become their leader in order to end the social discord which threatened to destroy them.

Canto XXIX

Still the Ninth Pouch of the Eighth Circle, among the Sowers of Schism and Scandal. The shade of Geri del Bello, Dante's relative. The travelers descend from there to the Tenth Pouch, reserved for the Falsifiers of Metals – counterfeiters posing as alchemists. The soul of Griffolino, punished as an alchemist, was also a pretender to magical power.

HERE IN THE POUCH where the sowers of schism are punished, Dante and Virgil have their first argument and their last. It is an argument about attention. Virgil takes Dante to task for staring too long at the sinners in the Ninth Pouch; Dante defends himself with the excuse that one of the sinners was of his own blood:

> '. . . In that cavern where
> I held mine eyes with such attention fixed,
>   I think a spirit of my blood laments
>   The sin which here below costs him so much.'
> Then said the Master: 'Do not let your thoughts
>   Be broken on him more from this time forward;
>   Attend you elsewhere, there let him remain;
> For him below the little bridge I saw,
>   Pointing at thee, threatening with his finger
>   Fiercely, and heard him called Geri del Bello.
> So wholly at that time were you obstructed
>   By him who formerly held Altaforte,
>   Thou didst not look his way; so he departed.' [18–30]

Never before has Dante given his attention to one soul (Bertran de Born, 'lord of Hautefort' [29]), and then felt that he should have been attending to another (his relative Geri del Bello); his attention is beginning to become divided.

> 'O my Conductor, his own violent death,
>   Which is not yet avenged for him,' I said,
>   'By any who is sharer in the shame,
> Made him disdainful; whence he went away,
>   As I imagine, without speaking to me,
>   And thereby made me pity him the more.' [31–36]

But it is better for Dante to leave the shade of Geri del Bello, better to leave him unavenged: 'He that loveth father or mother more than Me is not worthy of Me' [Matt. 10:37]. Dante, however, feels both pity and shame before the accusing finger of the shade, his murdered relative. Here we encounter the infernal principle of the *vendetta*, the blood feud, which is based on a kind of inner schism. The principle of the blood feud divides the love of Justice—which is what attracts Dante—from its impersonal roots in the metaphysical order. It renders the virtue of Justice interested and personalistic, and thereby perverts it for evil ends. On the psychological level, this schism results in a condition of split attention: whenever someone involved in a blood feud thinks of a person he loves, he is simultaneously forced to think of a person he hates, and vice versa. Here Dante implicitly criticizes the institution of the *vendetta*, while admitting its hold on him.

In this CANTO the Alchemists and Falsifiers of Coins are punished. Implicit in this sin is the degradation of knowledge from the sacred to the profane. As long as knowledge is sacred it remains open to higher realms, and stays within certain limits on the terrestrial plane; it doesn't descend into the worship technique for technique's sake. It was not any lack of ability or of psychological maturity, for example, that caused the Chinese to restrict the uses of gunpowder for centuries to ritual and amusement. As Frithjof Schuon points out,

Attempts which, in antiquity and the Middle Ages, which came nearest to mechanical inventions were those that served chiefly for amusement and were regarded as curiosities and thus as things which became legitimate by very reason of their exceptional character. The ancients were not like feckless children who handle everything within reach, but on the contrary like men of ripe judgment who avoid certain orders of possibilities, the disastrous consequences of which they foresee.[1]

The Falsifiers of Metals—counterfeiters posing as alchemists—represent the falsification of *human vocations* at their spiritual root. Every craft, in Dante's time, was controlled by a guild that was placed under the tutelage of a particular saint, thus demonstrating the spiritual or archetypal roots of the idea of 'vocation', according to which one is 'called' by God to a particular path in life. To be honest is not to pretend to be something one isn't, but to be the person one is really called to be. The initiated member of a craft guild was beholden, in theory at least, to something higher than social or commercial standards, since every craft was considered symbolic of a particular spiritual truth—which is why Dante calls this last pouch of Malebolge a 'cloister', and its inmates 'lay brothers' [40–41]. Skill is neutral, morally speaking—though it may symbolize higher realities—but honesty is not.

> *I saw two sitting propped against each other,*
>   *As pan is leaned on pan while they are heating,*
>   *From head to foot all spotted over with scabs;*
> *And I never saw a currycomb worked more quickly*
>   *By stable-boy for whom his master waits,*
>   *Or by one who keeps awake unwillingly,*
> *As they attacked themselves with clawing nails;*
>   *Their itching such great force and fury had*
>   *That for relief there was no other help.*
> *And the nails downward with them dragged the scab,*
>   *Just like a knife is used for scaling carp,*
>   *Or another fish with even bigger scales.* [73–84]

The souls of the Falsifiers tear at themselves; since they have 'aped nature' instead of working in line with her laws, they cannot accept

---

1. *Castes and Races*, (Ghent, NY: Sophia Perennis, 1982), p22, n10.

themselves for who they are. That they are constantly peeling scabs off their skin symbolizes the destructive revelation of an inner reality that should be kept hidden. And in its distorted resemblance to molting or a shedding of the skin it is also a parody of spiritual regeneration; one of the things the alchemists claimed to be able to produce, by means of their *elixir*, was the renewal of youth—one more example of the outer parody of an inner spiritual transformation.

> *Wholly did the good master draw close to me,*
>   *Saying: 'Say to them whatever you may wish.'*
>   *And I began, since he would have it so:*
> *'So that the memory of you may not fade*
>   *In the first world from out the minds of men,*
>   *But rather may survive under many suns,*
> *Say to me who ye are, and of what people. . . .'* [100–106]

Here Dante ironically appeals to these sinners' desire for worldly fame—as if the fame of the damned were not in reality the greatest shame conceivable. The soul who answers Dante's call is that of Griffolino of Arezzo:

> *'I of Arezzo was,' one made reply,*
>   *'And Albert of Siena had me burned;*
>   *But what I died for does not bring me here.*
> *'Tis true I said to him, speaking in jest,*
>   *That I could rise by flight into the air,*
>   *And he who had conceit, but little wit,*
> *Would have me show to him this art; and only*
>   *Because no Daedalus I made him, made me*
>   *To be burned by one who held him as his son.*
> *But to the final pouch of all the ten*
>   *For alchemy, which in the world I practised,*
>   *Minos, who cannot err, has me condemned.'* [109–120]

Griffolino was burned by the Bishop of Siena for claiming to be able to teach the bishop's protégé, Alberto of Siena, how to fly. He was executed for this false claim, which could also be looked at as a mere failure of skill, since if he had actually succeeded in constructing the first one-man glider, for example, he might possibly have saved his life and become famous. But he was damned for his practice of alchemy, here assumed by Dante to be an inherently false art (unlike sorcery, for example, which he would have recognized as a real art, albeit a demonic one). Griffolino was executed for a crime of the outer man, but damned for a sin that affected the inner one. His pretense of being able to teach people to fly manifests the sort of spiritual inflation or *hubris* that is visible to all, while hidden in his soul was a much more serious transgression, the sin of pseudo-alchemy, a counterfeit of inner spiritual transformation. And it was this inner falsification-of-soul that led him to the outer practice of deception—as is the case with so many false spiritual teachers, who claim to be able to teach their pupils to 'fly' spiritually, and some-time even physically.[2] Inner falsification is worse than social deception; the charisma required to deceive others on the social plane is here shown to be derived from an inner falsification of the soul in its relationship to God.

Though the power of alchemy to physically transform metals may be illusory—and if genuine, extremely rare—alchemy as an inner practice has been a valid spiritual method within Taoism, Islam and Christianity as well. The craft of alchemy, as one of the lesser mysteries, represents a return to primordiality, a restoration of the state of humanity before the fall. In Eden the crafts were unnecessary; according to the testimony of tradition, they were given to man by God to compensate for his loss of the Earthly Paradise. This return to primordiality through craft is represented by the 'seed of ants' in line 64. When Juno struck Aegina with a plague that destroyed nearly all living things, Jupiter re-populated the island by turning ants into men. These were the *Myrmidons*, a symbol of primordial 'earth-born' humanity, and of the crafts as well: there are no greater craftsmen in the animal kingdom than the ants.

2. In our time, Maharishi Mahesh Yogi has made the same claim; one of the courses available (or once available) through his organization purports to teach students how to levitate.

That Dante tells this story [58–64] suggests he may have known that there is more to *true* alchemy than the mere manipulation of appearances.[3]

In lines 125–132, Dante lists the members of the Spendthrift Club, a group of young noblemen of Siena, known for their vanity and profligacy, who made a point of squandering their estates and ended as objects of ridicule. Worldly vanity is a parody of true spirituality; the ego claims for itself what is due to the *Imago Dei*. The sin of the Spendthrifts is a kind of overflow from the graver sins of pseudo-alchemy, magical flight and spiritual fraud—like the *bombast* (pretentious, inflated writing or speech) that flowed from the soul of the alchemist Theophrastus Bombastus Von Hohenheim, whom we know as Paracelsus. A false spiritual teacher is one who deeply diverts the energy of the community soul from legitimate pursuits; the squandering of resources by the young aristocrats of the Spendthrift Club suggests the squandering of spiritual potential—perhaps through the belief, which we would today classify as 'New Age,' that Divine All-Possibility can be expressed in the outer, material world.

This is the point in the *Inferno* where Dante is most intensely assaulted by *pity* [36, and 43–45]. This is due to the fact that people who have the power to falsify the soul on this deep a level often show the kind of *charm* that can draw pity out of a stone—a pity that these souls in no way deserve. [See note 2, p 23]

---

3. See René Guénon, *The Esoterism of Dante* (Hillsdale, NY: Sophia Perennis, 2004), chap. 3, 'Masonic and Hermetic Parallels'.

Canto XXX

Still the Tenth Pouch of the Eighth Circle: the Falsifiers of Persons (the Impersonators); the Falsifiers of Coins (the Counterfeiters); the Falsifiers of Words (the Liars).

THE HIERARCHY OF FALSIFICATIONS analyzed and punished in the Tenth Pouch, each of which is worse than the one before, is as follows: The *impersonators*, those who falsify the body, are related to the physical plane; the *counterfeiters*, who falsify coins—values, that is, particularly emotional values or desires—are operating on the psychic plane; and the *falsifiers of language*, those who pervert meaning itself, have attempted to attack the Spiritual plane. Each level of falsification is more collective than the one before it. Impersonation affects only isolated individuals; the falsification of coins affects society more widely; the falsification of language affects every human being who speaks or thinks, distorting the world-view of an entire culture.

CANTO XXX has to do with disguise, cruelty, and fascination as the result of cruelty. The CANTO begins with the story of Athamas and Ino:

> '*Twas at the time when Juno was enraged*
> > *Through Semele against all the Theban blood,*
> > *As she already more than once had shown,*
> *So insane did Athamas become,*
> > *That, catching sight of his wife with their two sons*
> > *Carrying one of them upon each arm,*
> *He cried: 'Spread out the nets, that I may take*
> > *The lioness and her whelps along the pass!'*
> > *And then extended his unpitying claws,*
> *Seizing the first, who had the name Learchus,*

He whirled him round, and dashed him on a rock;
And she, still carrying the other, drowned herself. . . . [1–12]

Athamas, like Dante a little later in this Canto, cannot see who is there beside him—his wife Ino and their children—because he is involved in a quarrel and blinded by it. Jealous Juno, the wife of Jupiter, makes Athamas mad, causing him to murder his son and drive his wife to suicide—but this madness is also an expression of his own jealousy. The secret of this tragedy is that Athamas is sexually fascinated with his sister-in-law Semele because she has been possessed and taken to Olympus by Jupiter: he is insanely jealous of their relationship, just as Juno is, and this is what destroys his family. He is angry with his wife because he is attracted to her sister.[1]

Jealousy—which in essence is the desire to be someone else—has to do with the displacement of the self in relation to the other, in an attempt to annihilate oneself on the downward path of nihilism and illusion. The jealous one nihilistically denies his own true self, rather than mystically annihilating it. He does so without transcendence, on the downward path, and so his self is still there—only now it is the self of another, and he is stuck with it.[2]

Jealousy is the satanic falsification of the teaching of Jesus, 'Greater love hath no man than this, that a man lay down his life for his friends' [John 15:13].

Next Dante tells the story of the sorrows of Hecuba, Queen of Troy. She witnesses the sacrifice of her daughter Polyxena on the

1. Jupiter courted Semele, taking the form of shepherd. Then Juno appeared to Semele in the guise of her old nurse. 'People aren't always what they seem,' she said. 'If he really is Jupiter, ask him to appear to you in his heavenly glory.' Semele exacts this promise from Jupiter, and he fulfills it—but when he does, she is burned to ashes. This, however, does not end their relationship, since Jupiter translates Semele to Olympus after her death, which is why Juno is still jealous. The story of Semele is another example of the falsification of persons. Juno impersonates Semele's nurse out of jealousy and deceit, and Jupiter disguises himself as a shepherd out of lust— but also so as to mercifully protect the human realm from being consumed by the Divine: God must veil Himself in order to appear in this world.

2. This may have been what French poet Arthur Rimbaud meant when he said '"I" is another.' As such, it is the satanic inversion of the Vedantic doctrine of *tat twam asi*: '*That* (the divine Self) is who you really are.'

tomb of Achilles, and later sees the unburied body of her son Poly-
dorus, and these sights drive her to madness: howling like a dog, she
throws herself into the sea and drowns. Hecuba falsifies her person
in response to cruelty. She turns into a dog, demonstrating how
cruelty destroys the human form, specifically by driving it into illusion. Hecuba is thus the symbol of denial, which cannot overcome
despair and cruelty because it cannot face them, and therefore takes
refuge in the *unreal*, which is the essence of evil.

> . . . *I beheld two shadows pale and naked,*
>   *Who, biting, ran berserk, in just the way*
>   *A hog does, when he's turned loose from the sty.*
> *The one came at Capocchio, and sank*
>   *Its tusks into his neck, so that in dragging*
>   *It made his belly grate the solid bottom.*
> *And the Aretine, who trembling had remained,*
>   *Said to me: 'That shade's Gianni Schicchi,*
>   *And he goes raving, tearing all who meet him.'* [25–33]

In this part of the Inferno, rather than being tormented by demons
the sinners torment each other. This conflict has to do with a denial
of the true self leading to a confusion of self and other. Hecuba
became a dog as the result of this denial; here Giani Schicchi has
become a pig.

> '. . . *That is the ancient ghost*
>   *Of the indecent Myrrha, who became*
>   *Beyond all rightful love her father's lover.*
> *She came to sin with him after this manner,*
>   *By taking upon herself another's form.* . . .' [37–41]

Lying and falsification build up the world of illusion, one of the
centers of which is *incest*. For the daughter to impersonate another
woman—her own mother in most cases, psychologically speaking—
in order to sexually possess the father is a form of self-love (cf. the
reference to 'lick[ing] the mirror of Narcissus', [129]), which makes
real love impossible. It is also another and opposite form of jealousy

to that expressed in the story of Athamas and Ino. Rather than attempting to transcend herself through self-annihilation, Myrrha tries to overcome her loss of true self through annihilation of the other, as if the other's negation would necessarily lead to the birth of the self. This negation of the other is even greater than that represented by murder. The murdered one, at least, had once been alive; in this case, however, it is as if the negated one had never existed: 'I am my mother, therefore my mother never was.' The story of Myrrha deals with the falsification not of mystical self-annihilation, but of an even higher station, that of spiritual death and resurrection. It presents the satanic inversion of 'He who findeth his life will lose it and he who loseth his life for My sake shall find it' [Matt. 10:39].

Incest is also a parody of the sacred marriage of God with the human soul. Father-daughter incest may in some ways symbolize this divine marriage, but what is possible for the gods, what is valid on the archetypal level, becomes criminal when acted out on the human plane. Incest is also related to *narcissism*: Once the other has been totally denied for the sake of oneself, the only love remaining is the love for oneself *as another*.

> *I saw one made in the fashion of a lute,*
> *If only he'd been cut off at the groin,*
> *Right at the point at which a man is forked.*
> *The heavy dropsy, that so disproportions*
> *The sufferer's limbs with poorly transmuted humors*
> *That the face and belly of him no longer match*
> *Forced him to hold his two lips wide apart*
> *As a consumptive does, who, because of thirst*
> *Turns one lip upward, the other toward his chin.*
> *'O ye immune to every punishment*
> *In this grim world, and why I do not know,'*
> *He said to us, 'look now, and pay attention*
> *Unto the suffering of Master Adam;*
> *While living I had much of what I wanted;*
> *Now all I want, alas, is one drop of water.*
> *The rivulets, that from the verdant hills*
> *Of Casentino pour down into Arno,*

With channels cool and moist before my eyes
Are always there; the memory of them racks me.
I am more parched by the image of those waters
Than by this disease which strips my face of flesh.
The strict justice that chastises me
Takes its cue from the place in which I sinned.
There is Romena; there I counterfeited
The coin imprinted with the Baptist's seal,
For which I left my body, burned, above.' [49–75]

Master Adam, the falsifier of coins, is tormented—ironically—by dropsy coupled with thirst. Because counterfeiters inflate the value of the basic medium of exchange, they are now bloated with water, which can still not assuage their thirst; what is necessary for life has been transformed into a curse. His disease [54, 69] causes his face to shrink as his belly expands.[3] To be deprived of one's face is to lose one's defining humanity; here the lower instincts, greed in particular, have almost totally obliterated it.[4]

Master Adam has depleted the substance (decreased the actual gold content) of the coins he has falsified. This indicates a skewed relationship to the substantial pole, the feminine principle of *materia*, here symbolized by water, which in Aristotelian terms exists in a polar relationship with *forma*, the masculine principle, represented by the image of John the Baptist. The image remains intact, but the substance of it is less than it should be; and this forms the basis of Master Adam's punishment: the constant memory of the pure, clear water he can never drink [64–67]. By depleting substance, he has put everything into the realm of image, which is all that *forma* can be without sufficient *materia* to incarnate it. John the Baptist used flowing water to purify souls from sin. Master Adam, on the other hand, tried to materialize and literalize the substantial pole, thus

3. A being with shrunken face and bloated belly immediately suggests the image of the *preta* or hungry ghost in Buddhist mythology. The *preta's* belly is grotesquely bloated; his mouth has contracted until it is no bigger than the eye of a needle. To the degree that his craving expands, his ability to satisfy it shrinks away.

4. An understanding of this truth caused the Prophet Mohammed to prohibit his warriors from striking the face of the enemy in battle.

preventing it from flowing; this is why his body is now filled with stagnant water. The real nature of Substance lies in its ability to reflect and incarnate spiritual form, as when the Virgin Mary says, in the Magnificat, 'My soul doth magnify the Lord' [Luke 1:46]. It is a much subtler reality than substance or matter as we presently understand them.

Water is truth—as when Jesus, who is called a 'fountain of living water', says 'I am the way, the truth and the life.' But Master Adam, who has betrayed truth, can only have the memory of water, because truth is alive only in the present moment. And since he has made the truth his enemy, it is precisely this memory or fantasy of the truth that drives his soul ever more deeply into illusion.

> '. . . Who are these two poor sinners
>   Who smoke just like two wet hands do in winter,
>   And lie so close upon you to your right?'
> 'I found them here,' he answered, 'the day I rained
>   Into this rocky chasm. . . .' [91–95]
> 'One the false woman is who accused Joseph,
>   The other, lying Sinon, Greek of Troy;
>   From raging fever they give off such a stink.' [97–99]

The story of Joseph and Potiphar's wife, though she is numbered among the liars, is also related to the falsification of persons. Potiphar's wife sees Joseph as someone he is not—someone who is interested in her sexually and is trying to hide his feelings; she falsifies his person by lying to herself about his intent. In exactly this way do the passions accuse the Spirit of their own concupiscence, falsifying the *Imago Dei* within the human soul.

Sinon, who built the Trojan horse and lied to the Trojans about his intent, appears among the falsifiers of words. Because he attempted to empty words of meaning, he is now thirsty—thirsty for the truth. Unlike Master Adam, he is so involved in lying that he can't even retain putrid water; his soul is entirely parched. This is why Master Adam taunts him by saying, 'And to make you lick the mirror of Narcissus/You wouldn't need many words as invitation' [128–129]. The Mirror of Narcissus is the pool where he fell in love with his reflected image. It symbolizes the illusion that oneself-as-other actually exists; and this is a total illusion. To lose consciousness of what is other than oneself is bad enough, but to identify oneself *as* the other is to prevent this loss from ever being redressed. This mirror is the false image of real water. The liar, however, can only lick the mirror as if it were made of glass. He can never drink the water of the pool, because he has pressed truth into the service of illusion, and so lost it forever. The Mirror of Narcissus is the web of illusion that is woven by lies. It seems to present a coherent picture, but the image within it is simply made up of disrelated fragments. Narcissus is blind to anything objectively real, therefore he must mistake his own subjectivity for the objective reality he has lost—and this is objectivity's final death: the moment such a person believes he has finally regained objectivity is, in reality, the moment he has definitively lost it.[5]

Here, in the pouch of the falsifiers, the sinners are forced to quarrel with each other [100–132] in order to demonstrate that illusion fragments everything, that it brings no wholeness, no peace. The root of illusion is the longing for a false peace in that which is essentially fragmentary. This is the truth of illusion which illusion exists to hide.

> *And just as he who dreams of his own harm,*
> *And who, dreaming, wishes it were a dream*
> *So that he craves what is, as if it were not;*
> *Such I became, not having power to speak. . . .* [136–139]

---

5. This perception of oneself-as-other leading to the final loss of objectivity is the exact inversion of self-transcendence as seen from a *jñanic* perspective, where what had once been one's subjectivity becomes objectified before the *atman*, the Absolute Witness, which Frithjof Schuon calls 'the absolute Subject of our contingent subjectivity.' In *Survey of Metaphysics and Esoterism*, he says:

> when the perception of the Object is so intense that the consciousness of subject vanishes, the Object becomes Subject, as is the case in the union of love; but then the word 'subject' no longer has the meaning of a complement that is fragmentary by definition; it means on the contrary a totality which we conceive as subjective because it is conscious. (p39)

It is impossible to wake up from a dream like this because all the clues that it *is* a dream are hidden by the desire that it *be* a dream. This is illusion in its most concentrated form: the attempt to hide in fantasy from the deceptions of evil instead of awakening from them into the Truth.

Dante's prurient curiosity about the sinners' quarrel threatens to draw him into illusion, which is why he has turned his back to his spiritual Guide. And excessive remorse is also a part of illusion; it is illusion's revenge upon the repentant sinner for having broken with it. (Recognizing the dangers of excessive remorse, certain Sufis speak of the need to 'repent of repentance'.)

Canto XXXI

*Descent to the Ninth Circle with its frozen lake. The realm of the
Giants. The Giant Antaeus lower the travelers into the pit.*

DANTE AND VIRGIL now enter the world of the Giants or Titans
(in Sanskrit, the *Asuras* or warrior-demons); 'from the navel down,
all of them are in the central pit, at the embankment' [32–33]. To
Dante they look like the massive towers of a city until Virgil tells
him what they are.

The Giants are the archetype of repressed passions, the beings
whom William Blake, in *The Marriage of Heaven and Hell*, called
'the Antediluvians who are our Energies.' They are so deeply buried
that it takes an adjustment of perception on Dante's part to see
them as they are—and when he does, terror strikes him. Part of
what keeps one from seeing these passions in their true form is a
deep instinctual fear.

The Giants represent instincts which are deeply repressed because
they are unredeemed—which means that their repression is, from
one point of view, a function of divine mercy. The Giants are next to
unknowable because they exist on the border of an abysmal form-
lessness. They are personifications of the dissolution of personhood
in proximity to the substantial pole; but since they retain residues of
individuality instead of completely sacrificing it in pure receptivity
to the Spirit, they are satanic.

The Giants represent the world of impersonal oppression via
falsity—a falsity through which the quality of unique personhood is
almost entirely destroyed. In their destruction of *forma* or quality in
the name of *materia* or quantity, they represent the most ancient
example of what René Guénon calls *the reign of quantity*; they are the
root principles of materialism. As such they represent a block to the

development of human potential in the direction of the human form. Since the instincts are so buried in them, so violent and so evil, in effect they are precursors of Satan. The Giants are *impersonal* falsity and oppression; Satan himself is both personal and impersonal.

Since the Giants are four in number, they constitute a satanic parody of spiritual unity and integrity, such as that represented in the books of Ezekiel and Revelations by the Four Living Creatures. They possess a kind of awesome impersonal grandeur, like the Tower of Babel; they are the image of spiritual nobility quantified.

> *There it was less than night, and less than day,*
> *So that my sight could scarcely move ahead;*
> *But I could hear the loud blare of a horn,*
> *Loud enough to make a thunderclap seem faint,*
> *At this, my eyes, turned back upon their path*
> *Were now directed wholly to one place.* [10–15]

Dante and Virgil are now entering a realm where it is 'less than night and less than day' [10]. Even though it is a privation of light, night is not without its meaning; in its terrestrial aspect it can symbolize the Superessential, as with the maiden Layla ('night') in the Sufi poetry of Nizami. But night in Hell can never have this quality, because form has broken down to such a degree that it is not even possible for the travelers to call the chaotic murk that surrounds them 'night'. The very cyclical form of night and day has broken down; night can never entirely obliterate daylight for the Giants, and so day can never come. Night is a symbol of spiritual self-annihilation, as day is of resurrection—but neither of these things are possible in Hell.

> *As, when the fog is vanishing away,*
> *Little by little does the sight make out*
> *Whatever the mist that fills the air conceals,*
> *So, piercing through the dense and darksome air,*
> *Approaching closer and closer to the shore,*
> *As error fled, great terror grew upon me. . . .* [34–39]

At this point Dante's journey through Hell becomes a true purgation, a clear foreshadowing of the *Purgatorio*. His consciousness is heightened; his mind becomes more penetrating; he begins to face his worst fears. This passage demonstrates that some of the deepest illusions of the human soul are based on a flight from fear.

> *. . . as on its circular parapets*
> *Montereggioni crowns itself with towers—*
> *In just this way on the bank around the pit*
> *With one half of their bodies towering up*
> *Those terrible giants stood, threatened still by Jove*
> *Whenever he thunders on them out of heaven.*
> *And I the face of one already saw,*
> *Shoulders, breast, and a good part of the belly,*
> *And down along his sides hung both his arms.*
> *Certainly Nature, when she left off making*
> *Such creatures as these are, did well indeed,*
> *Depriving Mars of such executors;*
> *And if of elephants and whales she doth not repent*
> *Whosoever considers this matter deeply*
> *More just and more discreet will hold her for it;*
> *For where the sharpest force of intellect*
> *Is added unto evil will and power,*
> *No rampart humankind can build against it.* [40–57]

The Giants no longer appear in the outer world of nature since the advent of man because their forms are too much wedded to those base, abysmal instincts which are below the threshold of normal human consciousness; in order to see them, the eye of a consciousness *higher* than what is normally human had to awaken for Dante.[1]

'Acutest reasoning' really is present in the Giants—an intelligence that instinctively and instantaneously reaches its goal, a kind of infernal cunning. The angels in Paradise do not reason; they know

---

1. Perhaps in our own time we have learned how to press these giants, the elemental energies of nature, the reservoirs of *potentia*, into the service of Mars, god of war—as witness the artificial element *plutonium*, named after the god of the abyss.

instantaneously, by the power of Intellection. The Giants, who are fallen archangels, know by a lightning-fast, instinctive cunning that is the satanic inversion of this angelic intelligence. Nonetheless, Virgil calls the Giant Nimrod 'stupid' [70]; infernal cunning, for all its deftness, really is essentially unintelligent because there is no humanity in it. Nimrod, the satanic opponent of form and unity, has allied his intelligence with pride, not love, and therefore lost it; this is why Virgil calls him stupid.

> 'Raphel mai amècche zabi almi,'
> *Began to bellow that ferocious mouth,*
> *To which were not befitting sweeter psalms.*
> *And unto him my Guide: 'Idiotic soul,*
> *Keep to thy horn, and vent thyself with that,*
> *When wrath or other passion touches thee.*
> *Look around your neck and you'll find the belt*
> *Which keeps it fastened, O bewildered soul,*
> *See where it where lies across thy mighty breast.'* [67–75]

The bugle blast is now revealed to be that of Nimrod, the hunter who built the Tower of Babel [Gen. 10:8–11; 11:1–8];[2] the word *Raphél* in the apparently meaningless string of words he bellows identifies him either as an inverted form of St. Raphael, or as the companion (suggested by the word *amècche*) of another Giant more properly to be so identified; the four Giants are thus revealed as Satan's archangels, and the blast of Nimrod's hunting horn as the sound of Gabriel's trumpet in inverted form. The trumpet of Gabriel announces the general resurrection, but given that Nimrod's bugle is sounding in Hell, it bespeaks not resurrection but perpetual death, and announces the coming passage of Dante and Virgil into

---

2. According to René Guénon, 'the foundation of Nineveh and the Assyrian Empire by Nimrod seems actually to have been a revolt of the Kshatriyas [the Hindu name for the warrior caste] against the Chaldean sacerdotal caste. Thence the legendary relationship established between Nimrod and the *Nephilim* or other antidiluvian 'giants' which the Kshatriyas also represent in ancient times; and thence the epithet 'nimrodian' applied to a temporal power which affirms itself as independent of the spiritual authority' (*Symbols of Sacred Science*, p134).

the Ninth Circle, where the souls frozen in the lake fed by the river Cocytus are immobile, like corpses. The attack of the Titans on Olympus, their attempt to take heaven by storm, has here been transformed into an even more hopeless desire to free themselves from the chains of Hell.

Nimrod, in his speech, is like a postmodern philosopher: one who, in an attempt to rise above all languages and escape the limits of meaning, has in fact sunk below them, into the incoherent.[3] His nonsense is not entirely meaningless, but since it has less meaning than would give it the right to exist, it saps the intelligence of whoever tries to understand it.[4]

Nimrod appears bound across the chest because his Heart was bound in this way all along; he is bound across the neck because he tried to gain power through the use of speech in opposition to the knowledge of the Heart. 'Out of the abundance of the heart, the mouth speaketh' [Matt. 12:34]—but Nimrod never sought to speak out of abundance of Heart. In the figure of Nimrod we are approaching a parody of Christ as the Logos, the Word of God.

The fall of the Tower of Babel produced the 'confusion of tongues' [Gen. 11:1–9] which symbolizes both psychic and social fragmentation. And as the confusion of tongues divides, so Christ the Word unites: 'and there shall be one fold and one shepherd.'[5]

---

3. One could almost say that it was Dante's Nimrod who 'inspired' James Joyce to compose his *Finnegan's Wake*.

4. According to Frithjof Schuon, evil, as 'the possibility of impossibility', is fundamentally absurd. It is *a privatio boni*, an absence of the Good, which is necessarily also an absence of the Truth. In *The Play of Masks*, Schuon says:

> God is Reality as such. But things are 'outside God'—all sacred Scriptures attest to this—in respect of contingency . . . the Sovereign Good could not be the content of that privative existence—or that abyss of contingency—that is evil . . . privative and subversive possibilities are not *in Deo* except insofar as they testify to Being and therefore to All-Possibility, and not by their negative contents, which paradoxically signify nonexistence or the impossible, hence the absurd. [pp37–38]

5. The fall of the Tower of Babel represents the humanity's loss of the Primordial Tradition, the unified vision of divine Reality—which, after that moment, could only be outwardly expressed through multiple and seemingly opposed revelations and religious dispensations. According to René Guénon, 'Babylon is . . . a

The Apostles' ability to speak in many tongues on Pentecost is thus the exact opposite of the confusion of tongues, and also its redemption. Pentecost is the birth of the Church, which is *One*, Holy, Catholic and Apostolic; *Ecclesia* is the polar opposite of *Babel*, which is thereby the *Anti-Church*—possibly an Old Testament precursor to the Church of the Antichrist.

> *Then he to me: 'He doth himself accuse;*
>   *This one is Nimrod, by whose evil thought*
>   *A single language no longer serves the world.'* [76–78]

We might say that the universal language of spiritual truth, the *Sanatana Dharma*, already existed implicitly, in the human substance and the symbols of the natural world, before the days of Nimrod. He, however, became *explicitly* conscious of this universality on the mental level ('evil thought'), the level of the ego, and tried to use that knowledge for power—the result being the destruction of the entire civilization Nimrod tried to build, and with it of the ability of the human race to communicate with each other on the universal level. Here again we can see how Nimrod is a foreshadowing of Antichrist.

> *Therefore a longer journey did we make,*
>   *Turned to the left, and at a bow's-length from us*
>   *We found another far more large and fierce.*
> *In binding him, who might his master be*
>   *I cannot say; but he had tightly bound*
>   *His right arm back behind him, his left in front*
> *With heavy chain, that held him so snugly tied*
>   *From the neck on down, that on the part uncovered*
>   *It wound as much as five full times around him.*

---

remarkable name, *Bab-Ilu* signifying "Door of Heaven"... but it becomes synonymous with "confusion" (*Babel*) when the tradition is lost, being then the reversal of the symbol, *Janua Inferni* [Gate of Hell] taking the place of *Janua Coeli* [Gate of Heaven]' (*The King of the World*, [Hillsdale, NY: Sophia Perennis, 2004], p69, n8). In CANTO XXXI, Nimrod is placed at the 'gate' to the ninth circle of Hell.

> '*This proud one wished to make a test of strength*
>   *Of his own power against the Supreme Jove,*'
> *My Leader said, '*whence he has such reward.*
> *Ephialtes is his name; he showed great prowess*
>   *In the days when giants terrified the gods;*
> *Those arms he raised he never more shall move.*' [82–96]

As Nimrod is bound speech, so Ephialtes is bound force; the one represents rebellious intelligence, the other rebellious will. He and Nimrod are mentioned as rebelling against and punished by Jove, not Jehovah; the pagan King of the Gods is the closest approach to an image of the Living God that is possible in the depths of Hell.[6]

After seeing Nimrod and Ephialtes, Dante ask Virgil to show him the fiercest of the Giants, Briareus, but Virgil points him toward Antaeus instead. Dante's fascination with the enormity of Briareus points to an incipient inflation. He is becoming all too impressed, on an instinctual level, with the tremendousness of the Giants, the awesomeness of 'the reign of quantity'. Perhaps he is unconsciously beginning to hope that they will make him a 'big man'; in any case he is not placing his full attention upon the spiritual Path. Briareus is irrelevant to Dante; it is Antaeus, not Briareus, who will aid him in his journey. 'Sufficient unto the day is the evil thereof'.

> *There never was an earthquake of such might*
>   *That it could shake a tower so violently,*
> *As Ephialtes suddenly shook himself.*
> *Then was I more afraid of death than ever;*
>   *Nothing had been more fitting than such fear,*
> *If I had not beheld those sturdy chains.* [106–111]

Unlike Nimrod and Ephialtes, Antaeus can both speak and move; it is a distant reflection of God's mercy that the travelers encounter a

---

6. Ephialtes and his twin brother Otus, in the war of the Titans against the Gods, piled Mt. Ossa on top of Mt. Pelion in an attempt to reach Olympus, making Ephialtes a fit companion for the Nimrod who tried to build 'a tower that would reach to heaven'.

Giant who retains these abilities even at such a depth. Here evil intelligence and power mysteriously begin to serve the good, helping Dante and Virgil to overcome the heaviness and blindness of Hell.

At this point in the *Inferno* Dante fears death more than ever before [109], because now he is coming to a new understanding of what Hell really is. It is at this exact point that Virgil begins to speak of fame [115–129], reminding Anteus of his illustrious exploits and telling him how Dante, through the *Divine Comedy*, can bring him the fame that the souls of the damned all long for—and this shows just how infernal the energies are which produce a desire for fame in the living, because it is at this precise point that Antaeus grips Virgil—and Virgil, Dante—so as to set the pair down on the frozen lake of the ninth and last circle of Hell [130–143]. Fame is a kind of horizontal immortality, entirely cut off, as Hell is, from the vertical dimension. True immortality is eternal; the false immortality of fame is temporally bound; when time dies, it dies. [See p 115] Dante would 'have wished to take some other road' than that of fame [141], but he could not avoid it because it was destined for him. By God's will he was 'gripped' by fame so that the *Commedia* could spread its influence throughout the Christian world, and beyond.

For Dante, the temptation to take refuge in fame is based on a flight from the fear of death.

Canto XXXII

The First Ring of the Ninth Circle, the Hell of the Traitors to their Family—Caïna, named after Cain. The Second Ring, the Hell of the Traitors to their People—Antenora, named after Antenor the Trojan, who betrayed his city to the Greeks.

> *If I had use of rhymes both harsh and strident,*
> *As were appropriate to that dismal hole*
> *Down upon which the other crags converge,*
> *I would press out the juice of my conception*
> *More fully; but because I have them not,*
> *I must now bring myself to speak in fear;*
> *For 'tis no enterprise to take in jest,*
> *To sketch the base of all the universe,*
> *Nor for a tongue that still cries 'Mama!' 'Papa!'* [1–9]

THESE REALITIES are inexpressible like those of the supraformal planes of Paradise, but for the opposite reason. To be true to his material as a writer, Dante has to maintain some degree of order and harmony; otherwise he would not be able to express anything at all. But in so doing he must gloss over the true chaos of the reality he is encountering, which is why he fears he has failed to do justice to his subject.

Unfortunately, in dealing with similar subject matter, modern and contemporary writing too often 'becomes what it beholds' [cf. William Blake, *Jerusalem* 30:54, E177; 32:9, E178; 32:14, E178; 32:15, E178]; it sinks to the level of the chaos and darkness it is attempting to describe, and thus become unintelligible Here the 'mystery of iniquity' is shown as essentially *absurd*; the attempt to make such absurdity intelligible is futile.

> *But may those Ladies now sustain my verse,*
> *Who helped Amphion to wall up Thebes....* [10–12]

Dante's true muses in the composition of the *Divina Commedia* are Beatrice, St. Lucy and the Virgin Mary; yet the nine pagan Muses are the closest he can come to the image and memory of these celestial ladies in the Ninth Circle of Hell. In mentioning the poet Amphion—the music of whose lyre, inspired by the Muses, moved the stones of Mt. Cithaeron so that they arranged themselves into the walls of Thebes—Dante is asking the Muses to help him tell the story of Hell in such a way that the evil of it may be safely contained within his great poem, not let loose upon the world. The stones are also the hardness of deep Hell; to even describe such depths, one must overcome one's own hardness of heart.

> *O rabble ill-begotten above all,*
> *Who're in that place of which to speak is hard,*
> *'Twere better ye had here been sheep or goats!* [13–15]

The souls here are called 'miscreated' because, in an attempt to re-create themselves through sin, they have corrupted the *Imago Dei* within them. Yet the word 'miscreated' clearly implies that they are in one sense 'Devil's spawn', eternally predestined to damnation. To say that it would be better for them to have been sheep or goats is to place them *below* the level where the redeemed (the sheep) and the reprobate (the goats) are separated in the general judgment, below the level where what is sown in life is reaped in the afterlife.

But to say that these souls are damned from all eternity is not, paradoxically, to deny that they possessed free will; it has rather to do with the ontological reality they represent. They have sunk to that level of being which embodies the 'impossible possibility' of eternal damnation. According to Frithjof Schuon, evil is an 'eternal possibility within God' by virtue of the fact that the Absolute is necessarily Infinite, and thus embraces All-Possibility, including what Schuon calls 'the possibility of impossibility'—not, however, by the privative nature of evil as such, which is intrinsically opposed to God, Who is Pure Being.

'. . . *Look how thou steppest!*
Take heed thou do not trample with thy feet
The heads of your tired, miserable brothers!' [19–21]

What a terrible irony to call these traitors to kin Dante's *brothers!*
Yet there but for the grace of God go Dante, and all of us.

. . . I turned around, and saw before me
And underfoot a lake that, frozen hard
The semblance had of glass, and not of water. [22–24]

The deepest pit of Hell is cold, not hot, because heat is the principle
of life, and Hell is opposed to life. No matter how tormenting a fire
may be, it still bears some relationship to life energy. Heat is life and
love; cold is lovelessness, which is also death.[1]

Livid, as far up as the place of shame,
Were those disconsolate shades within the ice. . . . [34–35]

These souls are frozen up to their necks in ice because they are more
directly under the power of gravity even than the Giants, who are
only immobilized from the waist down. In them the lower aspects
of the soul are perpetually cut off from their consciousness; they
can never contact those part of them that hold them frozen in Hell.
They are fixed at too low a point for us even to be able to speak of
the perversion of the higher faculties in relation to them. Here the
lower aspects of the soul are, as it were, absolutized; the souls of the

---

1. According to Emanuel Swedenborg, 'The reason why the Sun [of the spiritual
world] appears before the angels' eyes as fiery is that love and fire correspond to
each other (*Divine Love and Wisdom* [London: The Swedenborg Society, 1987],
p 87). And in the words of René Guénon,

> Plutarch writes that the Sun, 'having the strength of a heart, disperses and gives out
> from itself heat and light, as if these were blood and breath' [*On the Face that Appears in
> the Orb of the Moon* 15:5] . . . if the 'breath' is here related to light, it is because it is
> properly the symbol of the spirit which is essentially the same thing as the intelligence.
> As for blood, it is obviously the vehicle of the 'animating heat', which refers especially to
> the 'vital' role of the central principle of the being [i.e., the spiritual Heart]' (*Symbols of
> Sacred Science*, p 400)

betrayers constitute a frozen parody of the adamantine changeless-
ness of the Absolute.

> *'Ye who so strain your breasts together, tell me,'*
>   *I said, 'who you are'; at that they bent their necks,*
>   *And when to me their faces they had lifted,*
> *Their eyes, which first were only moist within,*
>   *Gushed over the eyelids, and frost once more congealed*
>   *The tears between, and locked them up again.*
> *Clamp never bound together plank with plank*
>   *So strongly; whereupon, like a pair of rams,*
>   *They butted together; such anger overcame them.*
> *And one, who had by reason of the cold*
>   *Lost both his ears, still with his face turned downward,*
>   *Said: 'Why dost thou so mirror thyself in us?*
> *If thou desire to know who these two are,*
>   *The valley whence Bisenzio descends*
>   *Belonged to them and to their father Albert.*
> *They from one body came, and all Caina*
>   *Thou shalt search through, and shalt not find a shade*
>   *More worthy to be fixed within the ice. . . .'* [43–60]

Here the two sons of Count Alberto degli Alberti, who killed each
other, appear—locked in eternal hatred. In life, one was a Guelph,
one a Ghibelline. These souls represent the archetypal war of brothers; they are indeed 'brothers' of Dante, since before his exile from
Florence he was a major player in the same conflict that consumed
them. Here Dante confronts the image of his own fear of being
locked in hopeless conflict, of being unable to escape, through all
eternity, from the person one most deeply loathes. The souls of
Napoleone and Alessandro,[2] locked in a conflict that both separates
and unites them, are like a satanic inversion of the non-dual reality
of the Godhead, attained by the transcendence of the pairs-of-
opposites. That Dante was a White Guelph, neither an extreme
imperialist (a Ghibelline) nor an extreme papist (a Black Guelph)

---

2. Astonishingly, these are the names of two of the greatest universal conquer-
ors Europe ever produced, one of whom lived centuries before Dante (Alexander),
and the other (Napoleon Bonaparte) centuries after his death.

foreshadows his ability to attain the vision of the non-dual God-head in the Ninth Circle of Paradise.

> '... *Thou ... shalt not find a shade*
> *More worthy to be fixed within the ice;*
> *Not he in whom were broken breast and shadow*
> *At one and the same blow by Arthur's hand. ...'* [58–62]

For any description of deep Hell to be faithful to the intellect, light must pierce through the darkness, just as Arthur pierced Mordred so that a wound of light appeared in his shadow.

> *... we were advancing towards the middle,*
> *Where everything of weight is drawn together. ...* [73–74]

Weight is the quality of all unredeemed psychic and physical matter. Sin is weight because it obliterates the higher, spiritual faculties of the soul, those aspects of us which, as it were, have wings. If the will is not conformed to the spirit, one of the primal symbols of which is lightness and the power of flight, it sinks to the point where everything is falling away from the Spirit by its own dead weight. Yet even matter is redeemed, when, through the medium of human perception, by the grace of God it enters into the light of the Spirit. On the redemption of matter and its potential divinity, the fathers have this to say:

> It is ... false to repeat the commonplace that it is in matter as such that evil resides. For to speak truly, matter itself also participates in the order, the beauty, the form. ... How, if it were not so, could Good be produced from something evil? How could that thing be evil when it is impregnated with good? .. if matter is evil how can one explain its ability to engender and nourish nature? Evil as such engenders and nourishes nothing. It does not produce or preserve anything. If it be objected that matter ... leads souls towards evil, how could that be true when many material creatures turn their gaze toward the Good?[3]

3. Dionysius the Areopagite, *Divine Names*, IV, 28 (PG 3, 792), quoted in Clément, *The Roots of Christian Mysticism*, p 218.

Just as the body of the Lord was glorified on the mountains when it was transformed in the glory of God and in infinite light, so the bodies of the saints will be glorified and shine like lightning . . . 'the glory which thou hast given me I have given to them' (John 17:22). As countless candles are lighted from a single flame, so the bodies of all Christ's members will be what Christ is . . . our human nature is transformed into the fullness of God; it becomes wholly fire and light.[4]

The fire that is hidden and as it were smothered under the ashes of this world . . . will blaze out with its divinity and burn up the husk of death.[5]

Traitors are placed in the lowest part of Hell because betrayal is the central sin of the Christian tradition, represented by Judas, who betrayed Jesus to his enemies, and to a lesser extent Peter, who denied him three times before the cock crew. In the pre-communion prayers of the Eastern Orthodox liturgy, the congregation vows not to speak of God's Mystery to his enemies, or give the Judas kiss. The worst betrayal is to deny the truths of God and so set up a parody of them—and this is also a self-betrayal, which is why Judas must commit suicide.

Here, in the Ninth Circle of Hell, is where *fame* becomes *shame*. The dark side of fame is that it puts the ego in place of the Christ within as a kind parody of Him, and in so doing turns the soul into a travesty of itself; this is the source of its shame. (As William Blake said in *The Marriage of Heaven and Hell*, 'Shame is Pride's cloak'.) This is the sin of pride, the chief of the cardinal sins. The proud soul is host to a vicious cycle of fame and shame: shame prompts the soul to deny it by seeking fame, but fame sought in this way only deepens shame, often prompting its votaries to shameful acts as a sort of ego suicide, like that of Judas—the very opposite of self-sacrifice and ego-transcendence.

---

4. Pseudo-Macarius, *Fifteenth Homily*, 38 (PG 34, 602), quoted as above, p 268.
5. Gregory of Nyssa, *Against Eunomius*, 5 (PG 45, 708), quoted as above, p 268.

Canto XXXIII

Still the Second Ring of the Ninth Circle; the story of the death of Ugolino and his sons. Cannibalism. Passage to the Third Ring, Ptolemea, reserved for the Traitors to Guests and named after Ptolemy, governor of Jericho under the Seleucids, who killed the high priest Simon, his father-in-law, and two of his sons after inviting them to dinner. The living damned.

> *His uplifted his mouth from his grim repast,*
> *That sinner, and wiped it on the hair*
> *Of the same head that he had ripped apart.*
> *Then he began: 'You want me to renew,*
> *Before I speak, the desperate grief that wrings*
> *My heart already only to think of it;*
> *But if my words be seed that may bear fruit*
> *Of infamy to the traitor whom I gnaw,*
> *Speaking and weeping shalt thou see together.*
> *I know not who thou art, nor by what mode*
> *Thou hast come down here; but a Florentine*
> *Thou seemest to me truly, when I hear thee.*
> *You must know that I was Count Ugolino,*
> *And this one was Ruggieri the Archbishop;*
> *Now I will tell thee why I am his neighbor.'* [1–15]

UGOLINO IS SHOWN gnawing the brain of Archbishop Rugierri, who murdered him and his sons. By this Ugolino is trying to annihilate all semblance of intelligence in an attempt to take refuge from his hellish torment in a deeper darkness, not realizing that, for him, the depth of darkness has already been reached. At the same time he is attempting to incorporate the intelligence of Rugierri by eating his brain—such is the quality of infernal contradiction—but the effect of this is simply to destroy intelligence entirely. The souls in Hell have 'lost the good of the Intellect' [Canto III:18]. Intelligence can no longer do them any good; it has been turned into a curse.

> *This one appeared to me as lord and master. . . .* [28]

For one's worst enemy to be one's lord and master is an image of being totally under the power of Satan.

Ugolino now tells the horrifying story of how Rugierri sealed him and his sons in the tower where they were imprisoned by nailing the door shut, and left them to starve. The night before, he and his sons all had nightmares about their coming ordeal; this indicates that they were already starving for spiritual nourishment.

> '. . . *without a word*
> *I gazed into the faces of my sons.*
> *I wept not, so turned to stone I was within;*
> *They wept; and then my darling little Anselm*
> *Said: 'You stare so, father; what is wrong with you?'*
> *Still not a tear I shed, nor answer made*
> *All of that day, nor yet the night thereafter,*
> *Until another sun rose on the world.'* [47–54]

The pity of Ugolino is a parody of true pity. Horror outweighs pity in his soul, just as the horror of Hell must outweigh our pity for its inhabitants: 'I wept not, so turned to stone I was within' [49]. Because Ugolino did not grieve for his sons, we cannot grieve for him. One can give of oneself in grief, but when the ability to give and grieve is lost, and relationships still remain, it is as if one were devouring one's suffering companions.

All grief must contain an element of compassion, even for oneself, but this is the death of compassion, because horror has triumphed over pity. The saint who cares for lepers, for example, must be proof against horror, while retaining the power to grieve compassionately.

Death by starvation is an image of the complete absence of love. When the basic inability to give and receive affection is frozen, one result may be the eating disorder known as *anorexia*, or self-starvation.[1]

'... [in a dream] *with sharp fangs*
        It seemed to me I saw their flanks ripped open.' [36]

'Both of my hands in agony I bit;
        And, thinking that I did it out of hunger
        Immediately they rose up and said to me:
"Father, we would suffer so much less
        If you ate of us; since you yourself did clothe
        Your sons with this poor flesh, it's yours to strip."' [58–64][2]

'... *two days I called them after they were dead;*
        Then hunger did what sorrow could not do.' [74–75]

Dante here implies that Ugolino practiced cannibalism on the bodies of his dead sons, which is also suggested by his gnawing the head of Archbishop Rugierri; he devoured his offspring in order to prolong his own life. When aborted fetuses are used for scientific research in an attempt to prolong the life of the living, this too is a form of cannibalism. In lines 4–9 above, Ugolino has foregone the natural instinct of self-protection in order to blacken the name of his enemy the Archbishop; here Dante is telling us that the sin of *backbiting* is also cannibalism of a kind, whether or not it is expressed openly. In this context, the following story is told of the great Muslim saint Jonaid [Junaid]:

A man rose up where Jonaid was preaching and began to beg. 'This man is perfectly healthy,' thought Jonaid, 'He can earn his

---

1. This is not to imply that anorexia is sinful, only that it is usually the result of some deep violation of love, such as incest or other sexual abuse.

2. Here, in a perversion of filial piety, Ugolino accepts a worship from his sons that is due only to God. It is He, not a child's parents, Who is the ultimate giver of life. For human beings to arrogate to themselves the right to terminate the lives of their offspring, either before or after birth, is to act out the belief that human beings are without immortal souls.

living. Why does he beg, and impose on himself this humiliation?' That night Jonaid has a dream that a covered dish was set before him. 'Eat,' be was bidden. When he lifted the lid, he saw the man who had begged lying dead on the dish. 'I do not eat the flesh of men,' he protested. 'Then why did you do so in the mosque yesterday?' he was asked. Jonaid realized that he had been guilty of slander in his heart, and that he was being taken to task for an evil thought.[3]

> *And notwithstanding that, due to the cold*
> *All sensation then departed from my face*
> *Leaving it numb as any callus; still,*
> *It seemed to me as if I felt some wind;*
> *Whence I: 'My Master, who sets this in motion?*
> *Is not every vapor stifled here below?'*
> *He said to me: 'You'll be there soon enough*
> *Where your own eye will provide sufficient answer*
> *When you behold the cause of this plunging wind.'* [100–108]

In the Ninth Circle of Hell we are dealing with the infraformal, not the supraformal, which is why Dante's senses flee him. His numbness is in line with the psychological truth that the perceptive power of those who have lost their ability to grieve, due to cold-heartedness, itself becomes frozen. Emotional frigidity is the satanic parody of spiritual impassiveness and detachment; on the mystical level, Dante's numbness is, in effect, Satan's counterfeit of the Cloud of Unknowing.

The infernal wind Dante now feels blowing from above, which will be revealed in the next Canto as fanned by Lucifer's wings, is a satanic parody of the Holy Spirit. On Pentecost the Spirit comes as a wind which blesses each and confirms the integrity of each—a quality symbolized by the tongue of flame which appeared above each person's head in the room where Mary and the apostles had

3. Farid al-Din Attar, *Muslim Saints and Mystics* (London and NY: Routledge & Kegan Paul, 1979), pp 206–207, trans. A. J. Arberry.

gathered [Acts 2:2–3]. In the same way, a good host will make *each one* feel welcome; he is not so much interested in the number of his guests as in their unique qualities. The cold wind of Satan, on the other hand, is indiscriminate.

The bodies of those sinners who were traitors to their guests are still alive in the upper world, animated by demons, while their souls are tormented by cold in the lowest circle of Hell, their eyes sealed shut with frozen tears. Since they had no room for guests in their homes—Fra Alberigo, during a banquet he was hosting, murdered his guest Manfred, and Manfred's son—they are now 'host' to demonic powers.

The soul of Alberigo appeals to Dante:

> '*Lift from off my eyes these rigid veils,*
> *That I may vent the suffering that fills*
> *My heart, before my sorrow reverts to ice.*'
> *And I to him:* '*If thou wouldst have me help*
> *Say who you were; and if I free thee not,*
> *May I sink to the bottom of the ice.*' [112–117]

Traitorous hospitality is the sin of pretending to be kind in order to be cruel. *Rudeness is courtesy* [150] in the case of such false hosts: courtesy to the guests who were betrayed. Here we are drawing ever nearer to the sin of Judas, who betrayed Christ at a *banquet*. As the essence of hospitality is Christian charity, the greatest of the theological virtues (1 Cor. 13:13), so the violation of hospitality is virtually the greatest sin. The sinners in this circle, blinded by their own frozen tears, are in effect forbidden to weep. The 'gift of tears' is a charisma of the Holy Spirit which is granted to certain saints; even icons and other holy images will sometime miraculously weep. The traitorous hosts, however, are denied this gift. Dante has a right to misrepresent his intent to Fra Alberigo because it is imperative for him to reach the deepest pit of Hell, and pass beyond it; he lies and breaks his promise in order to protect his own spiritual journey, which takes precedence over all other considerations. Compassion is beautiful, but to have had compassion on this soul would have been misguided on Dante's part, because Fra Alberigo is beyond compassion. His soul is so deeply damned that that weeping could only further damage it, not relieve it. He has sunk below repentance, and so tears, in his case, can have only a negative meaning.

> *'In moat above,' said he, 'of Malebranche,*
> *There where is boiling the tenacious pitch,*
> *As yet had Michel Zanche not arrived,*
> *When this one left a devil in his stead*
> *Inside his body, and body of a kinsman*
> *Who together with him accomplished the betrayal.*
> *Now reach out with your hand, and do it quickly;*
> *Open my eyes'—but open them I did not....*[142–150]

Dante breaks his promise to Fra Alberigo, and reaps the consequences he has laid upon himself: he goes to the bottom of the ice, which is his actual goal. Dante refuses to regard the blind soul of Fra Alberigo in order to show us that to do so would be to misplace the virtue of courtesy, and therefore violate it. We should *grant no rights* to heartlessness and spiritual blindness, beyond the attention that a thorough examination of conscience requires, lest we become blind ourselves. Here we have an application appropriate to Hell of the dictum of the Hindu *rishis*, often quoted by Frithjof Schuon: 'There is no right superior to that of truth.'

Canto XXXIV

The Fourth and Last Ring of the Ninth Circle—Judecca, reserved for the Traitors against Benefactors, and named after Judas, who betrayed Christ. The vision of the three-headed Lucifer; Judas and the two murderers of Julius Caesar, Brutus and Cassius, eternally chewed in his three mouths. The passage through the center-point of darkness, and ascent to the earth's surface. Dante and Virgil again see the stars.

> 'Vexilla Regis prodeunt Inferni [the banners of the
>   King of Hell draw closer]
>   *Towards us; therefore look you up ahead,'*
>   *My Master said, 'and say if you can see him.'*
> *As, when there breathes a heavy fog, or when*
>   *Our hemisphere is darkening into night,*
>   *Appears far off a mill the wind is turning,*
> *Methought that such a building then I saw.* . . . [1–7]

SATAN FIRST APPEARS to Dante as something like a windmill because just as a windmill captures the wind, symbolic of the Spirit, and applies its power to work, so Satan steals the power of the Spirit and applies it to evil. Yet Satan only appears to possess independent power; insofar as he is like a windmill, he is entirely passive: it is the wind who moves him, not he the wind. This is another way of saying that, in the final analysis, nothing happens that is not God's will.

> *Now was I, and with fear in verse I put it,*
>   *Come to where the shades were wholly covered;*
>   *They glimmered through like wisps of straw in glass.* [10–12]

The souls in Judecca, the lowest ring of the Ninth Circle, are entirely buried in ice; theirs is truly a living death. These are the ones who did not simply steal the good from others and then go their own way, but actively returned evil for good. They actually punished others for doing good to them—and this kills life completely.

Satan's endless grinding of the three Traitors is a parody of the sacrament of the Eucharist. The faithful incorporate the Body of Christ in order to be incorporated into His Body, whereas Satan chews Judas, Brutus and Cassius endlessly without swallowing them, so as to perpetuate division forever. That the proverbially 'lean and hungry' Cassius [see Shakespeare, *Julius Caesar*] is called 'robust' by Dante in line 67 is a final piece of irony; it is as if Cassius, who thought he could grow fat through an act of treachery—in effect, by *eating* Caesar—is now eaten up by his own treachery until the end of time.

> *How frozen and powerless did I then become,*
> *Ask it not, Reader, for I write it not,*
> *Because all words would never be enough.*
> *I did not die, nor did I remain alive;*
> *Think for yourself, if you possess the wit,*
> *What I became, deprived of both death and life.* [22–27]

After the travelers pass through the 'center of gravity' represented by the body of Lucifer, it is as if the part of Lucifer that was dead is now alive, and that which was alive in him is now dead—hence Dante's description of his terrified reaction upon first seeing the Evil One.

If Lucifer were really dead, he could then be resurrected; but since he is not truly dead, he can never return to life. The quality of Lucifer is thus the reverse of the quality embodied in the sacrament of Baptism: to be immersed in the baptismal waters is to die in order to live. In this he is an apt symbol of Frithjof Schuon's doctrine that evil is the 'possibility of impossibility,' which is worth quoting at some length, now that we have reached the Ninth Circle of Hell:

The Absolute by definition includes the Infinite—their common content being Perfection or the Good—and the Infinite in its turn gives rise, at the degree of that 'lesser Absolute' that is Being, to ontological All-Possibility. Being cannot include efficient

Possibility, because it cannot prevent the Absolute from including the Infinite.

Possibility has so to speak two dimensions, one 'horizontal' and one 'descending,' or one 'qualitative' and the other 'quantitative,' analogically or metaphorically speaking. The first contains the indefinitely diverse qualities and archetypes, whereas the second projects them in the direction of 'nothingness' or impossibility. In drawing away from its source—namely pure Being—the second dimension on the one hand coagulates the qualities and archetypes, and on the other manifests their contraries; whence ultimately the phenomenon of contrastive manifestation, and consequently of evil. Being, which coincides with the personal God, cannot prevent evil because, as we have said, it cannot abolish, and could not wish to abolish, the Infinitude of the pure Absolute.

And this resolves the following difficulty; if God is both good and omnipotent, why does He not abolish evil? Does He not wish to, or can He not do so? For the reasons we have just indicated, He cannot abolish evil as such—and he does not wish to abolish it because He knows its metaphysical necessity—but He is able and wishes to abolish particular evils, and in fact, all particular evils are transient; the cosmogonic unfolding [which is not evil in itself but makes evil manifestations possible] itself is transient since universal manifestation is subject to phases and becomes reabsorbed 'periodically' into the Apocatastasis of the 'Night of Brahman'.

In one sense, the Absolute is beyond good and evil, but in another sense it is the very essence of goodness, which is to say that It is the Good as such. It is neither good nor evil insofar as It conditions, by the radiation of Its Infinitude, the genesis of what we term evil, but it is good in the sense that every conceivable good testifies to Its essential nature; evil as such could not have its roots in the pure Absolute, nor in that 'lesser Absolute' that is Being, the personal God. Moreover, evil ceases to be evil when it is seen as a metaphysical necessity contributing to that 'greater good' which is, on the one hand, the contrastive manifestation of the good, and on the other the reabsorption that transforms every evil into the Good which is both its origin and end; *ad majorem Dei gloriam*. As regards the root of the problem, we could also express ourselves as follows: the absolute Good has no opposite; a good that has an opposite is not the absolute good; 'God alone is good'.[1]

Now come face-to-face with Lucifer, Dante says:

> *Were he once as fair, as now he's foul,*
> *And still lifted up his brows against his Maker,*
> *Well may he be the source of every sorrow.* [34–36]

The source of all sorrow is the lack of gratitude, and the most fundamental form of ingratitude is not to be thankful for the gift of one's own existence. Ingratitude is based on the delusion that we are self-created; and this is the deepest delusion of all.

> *O, what a marvel it appeared to me,*
> *When I beheld three faces on his head!*
> *The face in front—that one was blood-red;*
> *The other two were joined together with it*
> *Just above the mid-part of each shoulder,*
> *All three were grown together at the crown;*
> *The right-hand one was somewhere between white and yellow;*
> *The left was such to look upon as those*
> *Who come from where the Nile falls toward the valley.*
> *Underneath each face spread out two mighty wings,*
> *Aptly proportioned to so great a bird;*
> *I never saw a ship with sails so wide.*
> *No feathers they had, but like those of a bat*
> *Their structure was; and all six he kept waving,*
> *So that, from them, three frigid winds arose;*
> *By those winds all Cocytus was ice.* [37–52]

---

1. *In the Face of the Absolute* (Bloomington, IN: World Wisdom Books, 1989), pp38–39.

As many have pointed out, the three faces of Satan are an infernal parody of the Blessed Trinity. And his six wings show him to be a fallen seraphim, who compose the highest of the nine choirs of angels in the system of Dionysius the Areopagite from *The Celestial Hierarchy*; in Eastern Orthodox iconography, the seraphim are depicted with six wings. The triplicity of Satan is based on his inability to attain unity, which is the same as his inability to be. The Unity of God, which is deployed as the Trinity, is above duality, but Satan has fallen below duality; he is fragmented in essence.

The three faces of Satan—one red, one black, and one a yellowish white—relate to what are called in Hinduism the three *gunas*, which are modes of *Prakriti*, the feminine or substantial pole, which is paired with *Purusha* ('person'), the masculine or essential pole.[2] Satan is thus revealed as the substantial pole in its most negative aspect; he cannot attain to form, because he has departed from his essence, but neither can he be freed from form. The substantial pole is a prison for him because he reached it passively, simply by falling that far. The wind fanned by Satan's wings is the freezing wind of hate, which appears in three aspects: wrath (red), lifelessness and false spiritual annihilation (black), and the deceptive pollution of spiritual truth (yellowish white); this is the infernal spirit that will produce and inform the Antichrist.

The pole of Substance in its positive aspect is none other than the Virgin Mary—she who is referred to in Genesis 3:15: 'And I will put enmity between thee and the woman, and between thy seed and her seed; it shall bruise thy head, and thou shalt bruise his heel.' As opposed to the rebellious passivity of Satan, the Virgin is the active receptivity of Pure Being, which draws toward it the Grace of God. That which is below all form by pure receptivity and perfect submission to God's will (pure *Prakriti*, that is, before it is divided into the three *gunas*), mysteriously mirrors what is above all form: the

---

2. The color of the *guna* of activity and expansion, *rajas*, is red; that of the *guna* of heaviness and stagnation, *tamas*, is black; and that of the *guna* of purity and elevation, *sattva*, is white—though here the yellow cast to Satan's white face shows that the principle of evil can do no more than present a counterfeit image of spiritual purity.

superessential reality of the Godhead, beyond Being itself.[3] Pure
Substance reflecting Beyond Being is symbolized by the Black Virgin, whose image appears both in Roman Catholicism and in the
iconography of the Eastern Orthodox Church.

> *As he asked me to, I clasped him round the neck,*
>> *While he watched to seize the fittest time and place;*
>> *And when the wings were opened wide apart,*
> *He laid fast hold upon the shaggy sides;*
>> *Climbed we downward then from tuft to tuft*
>> *Between the thick hair and the frozen crust.*
> *When we came down to where the thigh is hinged*
>> *Right at the thickest portion of the hip,*
>> *My Guide, with labor and with hard-drawn breath,*
> *Turned round his head to where his legs had been,*
>> *And grappled to the hair, as one who climbs,*
>> *So I thought that we were turning back to Hell.*
> *'Keep fast thy hold, for by such stairs as these,'*
>> *The Master said, panting as one fatigued,*
>> *'Must we take our leave of so much evil.'*
> *Then through the opening of a rock he passed,*
>> *And seated me upon the edge of it;*
>> *He came toward me then with firm and steady steps.*
> *I lifted up mine eyes and thought to see*
>> *The part of Lucifer that I had passed;*
>> *But I beheld him with his legs turned up.*
> *And if I then became disquieted,*
>> *Let thick-witted people wonder, who cannot see*
>> *What that point is which I had passed beyond.* [70–93]

3. According to William Blake in *The Four Zoas*, Satan is hermaphroditic:
'...hiding a Male within as in a Tabernacle, Abominable, Deadly' (VIII:103–106);
'...a male without a female counterpart...yet hiding the shadowy female Vala as
in an ark & Curtains' (VIII:248–255). Vala, as Goddess of Nature, is analogous to the
substantial pole or *Prakriti*—which, in retaining an ego of its own, in refusing to
submit to the Spirit, becomes satanic. It is as if Satan, in repressing femininity, has
failed to *attain* it.

First descending the body of Satan and then climbing upward toward his feet, the travelers pass the center of the universe without changing direction; their change is rather one of orientation. First the torso of Satan appears free of the ice of Cocytus, and his lower parts frozen solid within it—but then the travelers find themselves climbing up his legs, which are now free of ice, implying that it is his head and torso that are actually encrusted in ice. As Dante and Virgil pass through the state called Satan, what was frozen and dead is discovered to be open and free, and what was seemingly alive and capable of motion is revealed to be dead: for them, the way *out* of the Inferno is no longer the way *back*. In order to free oneself from Hell, Dante is saying, one must turn completely around without changing direction. It is a change of perspective that is required, and for this one can no longer depend upon one's past experience. This is the meaning of *metanoia*: 'be ye transformed by the renewing of your mind' [Rom. 12:2]. In the upper circles of Hell, it is as if one could retrace one's steps—except for the fact that, due to lack of character, no-one ever does—while in the lower circles, it is as if one might actually have the character necessary to turn back, except for the fact that circumstances now prevent it: if age only had strength, if youth only had wisdom, one might turn around and walk straight back out of Hell. That this is in fact impossible is foreshadowed by the figure of the Medusa in CANTO IX. And that the way out of Hell is not the way back through the realm of evil is a reflection and foreshadowing of the forgiveness of sins.

The central tyranny of the Ninth Circle of Hell is terror—terror at the sight of Lucifer. Usually when a soul is confronted with such terror it freezes, which is precisely what has happened to the souls in this circle. Evil is a privation of reality which nonetheless exists, in a sense, since it produces real effects. It is both real and unreal, and this is what leads those under its power to deny it. Whoever denies evil becomes terrified by it, and whoever is terrified by it rushes to deny it. Dante and Virgil, however, have spent their whole time in the Inferno *facing* evil, not denying it. To face it is to understand it, and what the travelers have understood is that evil is so lacking in positive good that it is essentially unreal; this is what gives them the power to escape from Hell by climbing the body of Lucifer.

Contrary to the condition of those souls who are frozen with terror, their knowledge of the unreality of evil lets them ignore its attempts to terrorize them, while their ability not to deny its existence allows them, by the special grace of God, not to perform it, certainly, but to *use* it. In the words of St. Silouan of the Holy Mountain, 'Keep thy mind in Hell and despair not.' Dante is demonstrating here that the *gnostic* way of overcoming evil is to face it and understand it.

> *There is a place below within that cave*
>   *At the farthest point beyond Beelzebub*
> *Which is not known by sight, but only sound—*
> *Sound of a little rivulet that descends*
>   *Through a hollow it has worn within the rock*
> *With a winding course, that by easy stages falls.* [127–132]

Salvation initially comes by hearing, not by seeing; through scripture, the word of God is heard by the human heart. The eye can certainly teach, but it can also inflame the passions, an aspect which led the Renaissance religious reformer Savonarola to preach, in Dante's city of Florence, against the vanity of the visual arts, at least when dedicated to vain pursuits. In *hearing*, the passions are put on hold, as it were; the will obeys on the basis of faith, without first having to know. *Seeing*, on the other hand, insofar as it is related to *gnosis*, has an esoteric aspect. As it says in the book of Job [42:5], 'I have heard of Thee with the hearing of the ear, but now my eye seeth Thee.' But here, in close proximity to Hell, the aspect of seeing, the esoteric aspect, must be carefully guarded.

It was in order to safeguard the esoteric dimension of spiritual truth that Judaism and Islam prohibited the making of any image of God, or of the human form. In light of this prohibition we can understand how the incarnation of God in visible human form as Jesus Christ is, in the words of St. Irenaeus of Lyons, a 'scandal'. The whole justification for icons in the Eastern Orthodox tradition is based on the mystery of the Incarnation; according to St. John Damascene in *On Holy Images*,

Of old, God the incorporeal and uncircumscribed was never depicted. Now, however, when God is seen clothed in flesh, and conversing with men, I make an image of the God Whom I see.[4]

In *hearing*, the true doctrine is addressed only to one's purity-of-heart; those who lack purity-of-heart will not heed. *Seeing*, on the other hand, is addressed to the entirety of one's soul. The one who sees the image of spiritual Truth is faced with all he is, including his passions. This ambiguous confrontation with both one's purity and with one's passions would seem incapable of saving the soul, but in fact it represents salvation in its deepest mode. Seeing, in the lower sense, relates to the passions, and also to the sensual world as composed of already-established forms; this is why the iconoclasts feared that the veneration of icons would lead to idolatry. But in the higher sense, seeing has to do with the direct Intellection of spiritual realities, with *gnosis*—as in the doctrine of the troubadours, for whom Love enters the Heart through the Eye. This higher way of seeing is related to what Frithjof Schuon calls 'intrinsic *bhakti*':

> The way of love—methodical *bhakti*—presupposes that through it we can go toward God; whereas love as such—intrinsic *bhakti*—accompanies the way of knowledge, *jñana*, and is based essentially on our sensitivity to the divine Beauty.[5]

The stream the travelers follow upstream, back to the earth's surface, is as if composed of the waters of both Lethe and Eunöe, the two rivers Dante encounters in the Earthly Paradise at the summit of Mount Purgatory, toward which they are now traveling. Eunöe is the remembrance of good, Lethe the forgetfulness of evil. The water of this stream is the contrary of the rivers of Hell; it is in fact the Mercy of God. Dante and Virgil could not leave Hell without at least a foretaste of the Earthly Paradise; after all their time in the Inferno, their spiritual effort is finally allowing them to ascend rather than descend, which is why they are pictured as moving directly, through

4. *Apologia of St. John Damascene Against Those who Decry Holy Images*, Part I; http://www.balamand.edu.lb/theology/Joicons.1.htm; paragraph 14.

5. *The Roots of the Human Condition*, (Bloomington, IN: World Wisdom Books, 1991), p 118.

space, from night to morning [104–105]. And upon setting foot again in what Dante calls the 'bright world,' they once more see the stars; their intellects can now, at least in potential, have access to the higher worlds.

Afterword

Purgatory as a Type of the Spiritual Path

With an Exegesis of the Second Canto of the Purgatorio

As MANY HAVE POINTED OUT, the Divine Comedy is a complete map of the spiritual life. In the *Inferno*, sin—both moral and intellectual—is discovered; in the *Purgatorio*, it is expiated; in the *Paradiso*, Divine Love leads on to spiritual Knowledge.

Of these three, the *Purgatorio* symbolizes the spiritual Path per se. This truth becomes clear in Canto II, where Virgil and Dante arrive in Ante-Purgatory at dawn, at the foot of the mountain which is Purgatory itself. As the sun rises, a boat full of souls, steered by an angel, glides swiftly across the waters. Among the souls Dante recognizes his friend Casella, the musician, who had set some of Dante's own poems to music. Casella is persuaded to sing, and all the souls gather around to listen—but then Cato appears and rebukes them for wasting time:

> ... *What is this, ye laggard spirits?*
> *What negligence, what loitering is this?*
> > *Run to the mountain, quick! Cast off the sloth,*
> > *That lets not God be manifest to you.* [120–123]

The souls, like frightened doves, begin their ascent.

✠

Dawn on the shores of Purgatory is initiation, the real beginning of the spiritual Path. As Venus rising in the first Canto is love, here 'Mars . . . conquered' [13–14] indicates love overcoming hate:

> . . . *as when, by morning conquered,*
>> *Through thick vapors Mars glows fiery red*
>> *Down in the West upon the ocean plain,*
> *There appeared to me—may I again behold it!—*
>> *A light along the sea so swiftly coming,*
>> *Its motion by no flight of wing is equalled;*
> *From which, when I a moment had withdrawn*
>> *My eyes, that I might question my Conductor,*
>> *Again I saw it, bigger and more bright.*
> *Then two white shapes that I could not make out*
>> *Appeared on either side, while underneath*
>> *Little by little another whiteness shone.* [13–24]

'See how he holds his wings, pointing to Heaven' says Virgil of the angelic boatman [34]. Both heavenly and fallen angels are 'birds' [37], but the wings of the boatman are pointed up: he moves by virtue of his relation to the vertical dimension.

Dante initially has a hard time making out the angel's shape [16–28]. His vision must *rise to meet* the angel; it must train itself to perceive the angelic realm. First he sees a light; then two 'whitenesses' on either side of it which he can't recognize; then another 'whiteness' below (possibly the angel's reflection, as in the engraving of this scene by Gustave Doré). It is only then that he recognizes the first light as the angel's wings. Dante must discriminate between substance and accident here—between the angel and his reflection—placing substance 'first'; this is all that is required for the accidental, the secondary reflection, to take its proper place, so it need not be explained or mentioned again.

As the boat crosses the water, the souls are singing the psalm '*In exitu Israël de Aegypto*' [46]. The Exodus is traditionally a symbol of the spiritual Path, and Purgatory is the realm of the spiritual traveler *par excellence;* anyone seeking initiation is asking to go through Purgatory in this life.

. . . he came to shore
In a little boat so very swift and light
That nothing of it could the water swallow. [40–42]

Water here is heaviness and instability of soul, the weight of unredeemed material nature; the boat is like the 'Spirit of God' that
'moved on the face of the waters' in Genesis. Redemption is implicitly identified with creation, as in the Catholic prayer, 'Come, Holy
Spirit, fill the hearts of Thy faithful, and enkindle in them the fire of
Thy love. Send forth Thy Spirit and they shall be created, and Thou
shalt renew the face of the earth.' The Spirit in Purgatory moves up
through all levels of the soul until the entire soul is purified.

According to Frithjof Schuon, Christianity, unlike Judaism or
Islam, is an esoterism preached openly to the whole community—
an 'exo-esoterism'. It is an initiatory Path, and the rite of initiation is
Baptism, or Baptism plus Confirmation (or Chrismation). Dionysius the Areopagite likewise identified Baptism with purgation,
Confirmation with illumination, and the Eucharist with perfection,
the three classical stages of the mystical Path. If a Christian is more
or less passive to the initiatory import of his Baptism, but is nonetheless faithful, he will not experience the fullness of purgation until
the next life.

Virgil and Dante, having passed 'alive' (i.e., consciously) through
Hell, are the *gnostics*—not in the sectarian sense of the word, but
rather those whose path to God is through knowledge. The knowers
arrive 'a little while before' [64] the pious faithful, but they too are
'strangers' at the foot of Mt. Purgatory [63], because the spiritual
Path is the one Path for all—something the heretical sectarian Gnostics denied. Yet the knowers, having had to do more conscious work
earlier on, find their later path easier; having 'taken up their cross',
they finally discover that their 'yoke is easy' and their 'burden light'.

On every side the Sun shot forth the day.
From mid-heaven with his well-aimed arrows
He had already driven Capricorn away. . . . [55–57]

Capricorn the Goat is like Lucifer expelled from Heaven; as the spiritual light dispels the heaviness of materiality, the residues are carried away by Lucifer, the scapegoat.

This is Dante's initial encounter with souls in purgation. The first soul he meets, that of Casella, loves him, and he returns that love. This is not quite the love of Paradise, but it is a love which extends beyond the grave. Love in Limbo is admiration; in Hell, pity; in Purgatory, true love; in Paradise, timeless love. The souls of the dead crowd around Dante when they realize he's alive:

> And as to a messenger with an olive branch
>   The people crowd around to hear the news,
>   And no one hesitates to join that throng,
> So at the sight of me stood motionless
>   Those fortunate spirits, all of them, as if
>   They'd forgotten to go forth and take their beauty. [70–75]

The gnostics bring the hope of consciousness to these souls; *gnosis* in its own way can also be a prayer for the dead. The olive branch, as a symbol of the peace of contemplation, represents the souls' hope for greater consciousness; the oil of the olive is a source of light. According to Tertullian, 'the flesh [in Confirmation or Chrismation] is anointed that the soul may be sanctified, the flesh is signed that the soul may be fortified, the flesh is placed in shadow by the laying on of hands that the soul may be illumined by the Holy Spirit.' But Dante, for those souls, is only the image of greater consciousness, not its realization; since they have become only partially conscious, the consequences of their former unconsciousness now begin to emerge, 'as if / They'd forgotten to go forth and take their beauty.'

As soon as the souls forget to pursue their course, they are ready to listen to Casella [106–119]. The poetry he sings is beautiful and has deep spiritual qualities, but it is not what they are there for. Casella's poetry reflects *gnosis*, but the people look at him in the wrong way; they pay attention to him instead of to the Mountain of Purgatory. This shows how *gnosis* should keep its own place and not distract simple souls; the gnostic above all should know where the Mountain is and not divert others from it. If the gnostic divulges the secret of his insight, he runs the risk of dazzling and blinding the simple souls—and *also himself*. In these latter days this secret must be divulged, however, which means that great and destructive illusions will necessarily abound. Through the celestial beauty of Casella's songs, the aesthetic dimension is parading itself before those souls undergoing purification. But because they contemplate this beauty as something apart from themselves, they enter into a spiritual stagnation which earns them the accusation of being 'loiterers'. Cato arrives in order to break this spell, so that they may go forth and become the beauty they are called to embody.

Dante attempts to embrace the shade of Casella, but his arms pass through him as if he were made of air:

> *O shadows—in all except appearance, empty.*
>   *Three times behind him did I clasp my hands,*
>   *And as often brought them back against my chest!* [79–81]

When the deepest form of truth is openly revealed, it is sometimes accompanied by the greatest lack of substance; this is the perennial pitfall of art and aesthetics. As with a great deal of latter-day 'esoterism,' the spiritual understanding is there, but not much real benefit is derived from it. The will is not engaged.

And so Dante ends in a self-embrace: art falsely worshipped, or esoterism wrongly lived, is narcissism; it is related to incomplete cognition. There is an attempt to mentally grasp the fruits of love and *gnosis* before having gone through the refining fires of Purgatory. In a story which appears in many traditions, a man destined for sainthood is seen with a glowing light around him. When told of this by the onlookers he is ashamed, and lets them know that this means he has not yet reached perfection.

Casella questions Dante:

> '. . . *Even as I loved thee*
>   *In mortal body, so I love thee free;*
>   *Therefore I stay; but why do you go on?*'
> '*My own Casella! to return once more*
>   *To where I am, I make this journey,*' *said I. . . .* [88–92]

Casella is saying: My soul has been saved without *gnosis*, without consciously traveling the spiritual Path—why, then, do *you* travel? The inner, 'gnostic' answer is that Dante, who as a gnostic is 'traveling' while still in the flesh, himself becomes the goal, in a certain sense, of the simple believer. To return to where one already is implies illumination. Because Dante is consciously returning to where he is, Casella can rest ('stay') in his presence, as if Dante were carrying the olive branch of peace. This reminds one of a statement by Martin Lings that

> all who pass through the gates of Heaven incur thereby a tremendous responsibility: it is henceforth the function of each to be, himself or herself, an integral feature of the celestial Garden, a source of felicity for all the other inmates, a vehicle of the Divine Presence.[1]

On the outer level, however, Dante is also saying that he must travel the spiritual Path in the flesh simply to be saved; if he doesn't go through Purgatory in this life, after death he will be damned. Greater spiritual capacity brings with it greater temptation: 'To whom much has been given, much will be required.'

When Dante asks Casella why he has been tardy in reaching the shores of Purgatory, he answers:

> . . . *No injury has been done to me,*
> *If he who elevates when and whom he pleases*
> *Has many times denied to me this passage,*
> *For from a righteous Will his will derives.* [94–97]

Here Casella is beginning to intuit, and rest in, a justice that is beyond his mere individuality. (cf. the *Paradiso*, CANTO III)

As the Canto ends, Cato the Younger arrives, provokingly and deftly awakening the souls from their complacency, reminding them that for the ascent of the Mountain of Purgatory they will need aspiration, zeal, and the fear of God. Cato, as a suicide—though for reasons of honor, not despair—may be one of those

---

1. Cf. *Symbol & Archetype* (Cambridge: Quinta Essentia, 1991), p53.

souls who must wait in Purgatory until the end of time, but he has as compensation his position as Purgatory's 'ruler'. The souls who must wait until the end of time to enter Paradise are those who lack the ability to transcend time through intellectual intuition.

When Cato appears, the pride of love is transformed into love in the mode of fear.

Feast of the Dormition, 2003

Printed in the United States
26577LVS00001B/261

9 781597 310017